Below: Hogans of logs and earth are winter homes for the Navajo. Seldom are more than two or three together. In the background, Lukachukai Mountains.

Right: Sandstone outcropping on Roof Butte (elevation 9808 feet). Lukachukai Mountain view with Kah-bihghi Valley and Carrizo Mountains in distance.

Below: A Navajo flock of sheep and goats grazing leisurely at the base of the Lukachukai Mountains.

Right: Aspen leaves carpet the forest floor in the Lukachukai Mountains, Navajo Indian Reservation.

Right: Moon over 7100 foot Agathla Peak will soon fade as the sun rises above the distant horizon.

Below: Cholla, Saguaro, and flowering Encelia dot desert slope above Salt River near State Highway 288.

Right: The Salt River flows along vertical rock walls and multi-hued salt formations in Fort Apache land.

Below: Watercress thrives in the gentle waters of Cibecue Creek on Fort Apache Indian Reservation.

Right: Desert Falls on Salt River in Apache Indian Reservation. Foreground, Prickly pear cactus, Sotol Yucca.

Below: Autumn hues intensify quaking aspens near McNary (elevation 7315 feet) in the White Mountains.

ARIZONA

A yowling knob of hellish fire drifts untethered in blue-black space. So solitary is this immense lump of boiling flame that it gives light and warmth only to itself and to the few poor droplets of its own cooled flesh whirling near.

In the snarling, rumbling center of this blistering ball of flaming gas, nearly half a million miles beneath its surface, 4.7 tons of matter are converted into energy each second. Cobbled with imperfections, raked by surface winds of more than a thousand miles an hour, pimpled with cold black spots more than thirty miles across and whiskered with prominences that tendril out two hundred thousand miles into the indifferent void surrounding it, this great furnace has been devouring itself with horrid violence for more than a billion years.

It is a star, one of ten billion like it in our galaxy; an ordinary, minor star. It is the one we call the sun.

At its raging heart the temperature is 35,000 degrees Fahrenheit; at its seething surface, 11,000 degrees. The earth receives about one and a half horsepower per square yard of solar energy, about one two-billionths of the sun's prodigious production. And for the next twenty-five million generations, as the sun exhausts its two million, million, million tons of matter, that solar energy will continue as the source of all energy, of all life on earth.

Only the astronauts have seen the sun as it appears in absolute space, but the most primitive races of men early understood that their survival was the sufferance of this hotly staring cosmic eye. At first the sun's power was invested with motive and called god. Shamash, Ra, Helios, Bog, Amaterasu, Frey, Rama Chandra, Ipalnemohualni: the sun deity wore a thousand names as countless populations of men begged forebearance from its evident but unfathomable influence over their lives.

The Chinese early recorded the sun's regularity and could predict eclipses, but it was the irreverent Greeks who secularized the sun in earnest. Thales, Philolaus and Hipparchus of Rhodes had correctly defined the nature and relationships of the sun, the stars and the planets a century before Christ. In the twenty centuries since, astronomers have accumulated whole libraries of information about the sun, and with each new fact painstakingly gathered and confirmed, the sun was stripped of a little more of its mystery. By the end of the 19th century the civilized world had lost its religious awe of the sun altogether.

Yet there remain regions on our spinning clod of mud where the sun is not easily dismissed as merely a natural phenomenon of great magnitude, where the sun, if no longer a god, is still a king, advancing in its daily progress with the pomp, power and pageantry of an absolute monarch.

Arizona is one such place.

In Monument Valley, as sunrise marks its first flourishing entrance upon the land, the sun reaches up from beyond the horizon to pierce the knobbled fissures of the Yebechai Rocks with solid sabres of streaming light before the sun itself explodes through the sandstone barricades to spring into the early morning sky. On hillsides sheep tiptoe daintily to be met by dogs that chivvy them back to their bands. A few nervous baa-baa-baas and the valley is awake. It is as calm and as serene as before, except that now Navajo herdsmen are stirring themselves in its cool vastnesses.

Not far away, campers at the Tribal Park headquarters at the entrance to the Valley are stunned awake by the shattering impact of the sun's light splattering between the sandstone pillars called the Mittens. As long shadows slip smoothly down the sheer stone walls of the naked red cliffs, the sound of rattling crockery drifts gently from a dozen camps and the aroma of coffee gives body to the morning breeze.

At Goulding's Lodge the dogs have wakended first, grumbling and snuffling as the sunlight coaxes their eyes open. As if on signal, a parade of towering monoliths trail out long black shadowcapes behind them to be nibbled slowly back by sunlight as the day unfolds.

At Grand Canyon, more than one hundred fifty miles to the west and south of Monument Valley, the autumn sun rises into a peach-pink and rose-yellow sky like a lemon-colored marble, as cool and as brittle as glass. Light enters gingerly into the hushed and windless depths of the Canyon, like an old man settling into a cold bath. The sun will have its way later when the spires and minarets of the Canyon walls splash its plunging light into a spray of vivid color, but at sunrise the light is frail and paltry against this abysmal seam splitting the earth's skin.

Far to the south the sun lunges up from behind the snaggle-toothed summits of the Ajo Mountains to hurl its sharp light vainly after the shadows that race to the lee slopes for safety. There they cling beneath rocks, scuttle into crevices and secrete themselves to cower, guilty memories of night, as the sun marches past overhead.

The newly risen sun bloodies the sides of Sunset Crater, silhouettes the Wukoki pueblo ruin as a fantastic desert shipwreck forever battered by jumbled waves of sandstone, and filters through a quivering sieve of leaves to gleam in the quiet pools and begin a day of basking on the water-smoothed rocks of Oak Creek Canyon.

A hundred yards from the Kaibab Trail in Grand Canyon a rock squirrel emerges from his burrow, scampers in short bursts to the spike-leafed base of a century plant, pauses for one long, frozen moment, then leaps for the stalk rising up from its center. Clutching at it as it sways from the impact of its leap, the squirrel gnaws at the juicy stem. From a nearby promontory the twitching of that single stalk in a forest of stationary plumes catches the attention of a gray fox, and he pads off toward it with apparent unconcern. When the squirrel at last succeeds in felling the succulent stem, and leaps to earth to drag it home, he becomes breakfast for the fox.

In the flat desert land around remote Palm Canyon in the Kofa Mountains, tarantulas have waited tensed near their holes all night for the maddening touch of an unwary insect. Dimly they perceive the sun through their eight blind eyes and end their hunting. Lifting their hairy legs in time to an otherworldly rhythm, they creep away in a slow dance to await the sun's departure.

In the volcanic domes of the White Mountains owls regain their perches clumsily, their hunting finished too, and hawks thump their wings heavily against the thin morning air to shove themselves aloft. In the streets of Phoenix, Tucson, Flagstaff and Prescott, automobiles are ferrying the first platoons of workers to their jobs.

Most work in Arizona is strongly sun-related. It is uninterrupted sunlight that permits from six to eight harvests of certain crops in several localities of Arizona each year and three to four in others. It is this sunlight that nourishes thirty vegetable crops, twenty kinds of fruit, and feed and seed crops, as well as cotton, the principal cash crop in Arizona.

Together agriculture and livestock account for substantially more than a half-billion dollars annually in the Arizona economy, but manufacturing accounts for more than that. And Arizona owes its industrial growth in large measure to the sun. For decades growing numbers of skilled, able men and women have deserted the deep-wintered east and midwest for the sun-drenched Arizona landscape, creating as a side effect a large reservoir of labor in the state. To expanding industry seeking new site locations, this surplus labor pool has been a significant factor in the decision to locate in Arizona.

And with an average year of more than 300 sunshine days, the sector of the Arizona economy which traces its vitality most directly to the sun is also the fastest growing: the business of vacations. Each year Arizona is besieged by swelling armies of travelers. They come to laze and lollygag, and to stare in wonder at the state's staggering physical beauty, but most of all to experience the effect on their exposed skin of the 0.29 calory of heat energy per square inch per minute cast upon the earth's surface by the sun.

In the morning summer skies clouds appear. Little white pufferbellies at first, they swell to impressive size, sides stretched as smooth and glistening as carved soap. The edges darken. In minutes the clouds are obese tumors blotting up the sunlight and wadding every crevice through which the sky appears. And then they burst, splitting open everywhere at once like waterbags, drenching the soil as they sail past. Within an hour the steaming earth has sucked up what moisture has not raced away down long-dry washes and arroyos, boiling with furious, muddy energy to nourish the rivers.

Summer's rains are gifts from the distant seas, products of the warm, moist air that slips like a fugitive around the edges of an Atlantic Ocean high pressure system and smuggles itself into Arizona by way of the Gulf of Mexico. When these masses of unstable air are roughed across the southern and eastern mountaintops like sopping coveralls over a washboard, rain crashes down with thunder and lightning. Other summer storms are imports from Mexico, products of tropical disturbances off her west coast which cross the border to spill down steady rains.

Winter's storms are seldom those received in other parts of the nation, for the storm belt of the middle latitudes does not often sag as far south as Arizona. Instead, billowing knots of cold, fretful air drift east from Hawaii and loiter over southern California for several days before being dragged up into the high northeasterly jet stream. Above Arizona these air pillows relax their grip on the chilly moisture carried in from the sea and let fall rain and snow in varying degrees of intensity.

Precipitation is niggardly at all seasons in Arizona, but it is stingiest in the high mesa country of the northeast corner, and in the lowland desert of the southwest. These regions are barricaded against the intrusion of moist air by brawny mountain ranges.

Because water reaches Arizona's surface so seldom, and in such small amounts, and because much of what does fall to earth is lost at once to evaporation, the climate is extremely dry, and the humidity extremely low. Only in the densely forested central mountain belt that separates the high mesa country from the southern deserts is the precipitation relatively heavy and reasonably dependable from year to year.

In the blazing heat of the lowland summer, shadows, dwarfed by the brassy presence overhead, tuck themselves deeper into places of concealment. Animals, even insects, go to cover, except that gaudy lizards dart and skip over the rocks in stupid recreation, their tiny minds excited to a frenzy by the merciless heat. One Arizona lizard lives in dune sand, and has feet especially fringed to speed his movements across his territory. Other creatures, too, have adopted special characteristics to cope with their hot, dry homeland. The kangaroo rat is one. He lives without ever drinking water; he extracts the moisture he requires for life from the solid vegetable matter on which he feeds by a highly specialized metabolic process.

It is well that they do adapt, for the penalty for the lack of this ability has been death or banishment. Ten thousand years ago, when men first settled in the sun's domain, they hunted mammoths, ground sloths, horses, camels and buffalo until their own prowess and the drying climate annihilated these creatures or forced them to more humid lands.

To survive the impact of the sun's overwhelming presence in Arizona's lowland deserts, plant life too has been forced to daring gambles.

The saguaro cactus, the sun's emissary in the south, sends roots braiding out from the base of its trunk in every direction, barely a finger's length deep in the sandy soil, to capture every molecule of moisture that penetrates the ground for yards around. In the hushed aftermath of a sudden summer shower, when the creosote bushes, their tiny varnished leaves washed free of dust, perfume the air with a rich turpentine scent, the cactuses gorge themselves with water until they bulge. The saguaro grows no leaves from which water might be lost by evaporation. Instead it hides its food-producing cells within the single trunk and uplifted arms where no pores can let the precious moisture escape to the wind. The saguaro's glossy skin is impervious to wind and sun alike, and it can survive an incredible amount of time upon its self-contained reservoir of water, even when separated from its roots. Other cactus species have developed thickly bristling spines which protect them still further from the burden of the sun's largesse by casting a soothing, latticed shadow grid across their glistening skins.

The ocotillo, too, has solved the problem posed by the sun. Its thin, thorny stalks rise up like a bundle of whips to twice the height of a man, but they feather themselves with leaves only briefly, in the spring, when they are required for the unfurling of bright red flowers from the tip of each nodding wand. The Palo Verde tree has leaves the year around, but they are so tiny in deference to the evaporative heat of the sun and the sucking winds that they cannot contain enough chlorophyll to sustain life. So branches and twigs take on this function, providing the graceful tree with a cool, misty, all-green cast refreshing to see in the desert floor.

Every plant in the desert lowlands bears evidence of bowing to the imperious demands of the sovereign sun. They are tough, these sun-baked vegetables, small and sinewed, sharply spined and often bitter to the taste. But few regions in the nation can match the type of Arizona's 3,370 species of plant life.

In autumn, midday sunlight seeps down the crenelated sides of Havasupai Canyon to ignite the cottonwoods in its depths like red and yellow bonfires against the shadow-patterned canyonsides. At Canyon de Chelly (de shay), in the heartland of the Navajo country, a thirsty band of sheep flows over the valley floor in a wooly flood and dams itself around a pool of water.

In winter, skiers glide beneath a cheerful sun, their bright clothing like moving mosaic chips against the snow spread across the side of Mount Lemmon in the Santa Catalinas. East of Yuma the sky is dank with clouds flung up like greasy rags to drape the sky. From above Kitt Peak an errant hem drifts down to snag on the mountaintop and leave it glazed with snow.

The afternoon sun in summer begins its downward journey like a sleepily blinking eye swabbed with cotton clouds. Already in the canyons and on the eastern hillsides shadows are moving tentatively out of hiding. At Grand Falls on the Little Colorado the river is still celebrating a summer thundershower hours after the event. Tons of muddy rainwater crash over the falls in bawdy violence to grind its bed microscopically deeper into the channel.

As day wanes, the sun descends with majestic languor beyond the Colorado. Desert animals brave the heat again. A gambel's quail, perched jauntily on a cholla cactus, calls with a low-pitched lament for a mate. Plume wagging, he repeats his giddy invitation before fluttering away alone. Above a pool of rainwater in the Canyon Diablo two thousand bats are flying madly in a squeaking, shrieking swarm. In patched and sagging Oatman a screendoor slaps shut at one of the miner's houses surviving in genteel delapidation so long after the mines have shut down. Parrots from Mexico chatter absent-mindedly to one another as they search the thickets of the remote highlands of the Chiricahua Mountains for prey.

In winter the sun sets early, its chilly rays illuminating the San Francisco Peaks, powerfully printed in black against the dove grey sky. All here is chilled, and the pearly smudge of sun gives no more warmth than a flashlight.

The autumn sun descends behind the Mission San Xavier del Bac like a heavy red balloon. At Easter the sun sets on Organ Pipe Cactus National Monument with such symphonic verve that the earth seems to tremble. Shadows as softly purple as a baby's blanket swathe the throats of Teddy Bear and Estes Canyons and rush out across the plains like floodwaters before slowly rising toward the glowing summits to the east.

And then, in the cloud-cobbled sky overhead, to the never-ending wonder of the crowds that gather at Organ Pipe, at the Grand Canyon's Hopi Point, at backyard barbecues in Phoenix and Tucson, at hundreds of places throughout the state, the vanishing sun scrawls its signature across the western sky: a miles-wide strip of psychedelic bacon, sizzling with all the colors of the universe. Gold, pale green, red, every shade of blue, bone white, orange, silver, salmon pink, violet, bright yellow, peach—the sun breathes them across the clouds in stately measure.

And at last the sun has dragged its trailing peacock's tail across the sky and gone. The earth is left in night, the single great shadow she casts upon herself. The lights of Arizona's cities glitter like beads. Coyotes skulk from their dens. Night birds take wing.

And then the sun, in a negligent afterthought that confirms its majesty, reaches back from beyond the horizon to knight the moon its seneschal.

Whereupon this pinchbeck viceroy preens itself in borrowed glory and grudgingly doles light down. For it is the singular duty of this silver bulb in night's black ceiling to hold the earth in thrall—with sunlight—until the king's return.

[THE HIGH MESA COUNTRY]

The high mesa country of northeastern Arizona is a layered accumulation of ancient sea beds and frozen sand dunes nibbled by eons of wind and rain into a lacy confusion of red mesas and gullies, of soaring gnawed-rock towers that erupt from the sand-flooded floor of Monument Valley like gargantuan stumps and limbless trees rising from a shallow honey-colored sea to glow pink and gold and ochre in the glancing light of the setting sun. There are mountains here, distant blue ranges capped with pine forests and seamed with antic streams, but for the most the land is lower, drier and less accommodating to sentimental notions of beauty. It is a fierce, broken land where streams and rivulets flow fitfully, if they flow at all, and the river beds, all but one, are dry. The wind-whipped, seared red soil is scarcely capable of nourishing the pinyon pines and junipers that are its most ambitious growth; the ground sucks into itself much of the moisture released by the melting of winter's snows, and gives it rapidly up again in evaporation. The rain that lashes down in furious thunderstorms is sluiced away in growling torrents of muddy water and tumbling rocks through the network of gullies that empty, eventually, into the Colorado River. This austere region of uncompromising distance and insistent color encompasses the ragged southern edge of the Colorado Plateaus Province and the desert that stretches away from its base south to the Mogollon Rim.

A thousand years ago this land was not so stark. Green grass was firmly rooted in the red soil that supports only scrubby gray brush today, and many of the present dry washes channeled trickles of flowing water. Where sufficient seasonable water coincided with fertile soil there were fields of corn and beans and squash with cities standing beside them.

They were prosperous cities, scattered through the maze of canyons and cuts in what is now northeastern Arizona, southeastern Utah, southwestern Colorado and eastern New Mexico, heavily populated by a highly cultured race of farmers, connected by ties of common tradition, languages and kinships, as well as by trade. There were hundreds of them. Some were small and relatively simple, others abandoned and empty because of local changes that had made them uninhabitable, and still more pulsing with life and the activities of hundreds, even thousands, of citizens. The cultivation of the fields beyond the walls of these cities was accomplished with a great expertness. The farmers used a calendar composed of the rising sun and the eastern horizon to mark the beginning of each growing season. Equally important, they had learned the ways by which to gain the cooperation of the spiritual presences which could bring them rain and turn aside the wind which whipped sand to tatter the young corn stalks and drifted it to bury the mounds in which squash was rooted. These people did not make the distinctions we do between the natural and the supernatural; the reality in which they lived encompassed them both and almost every activity of daily life was ritualized, or affected by ritual in order to gain the cooperation of the spiritual forces governing the world.

In addition to the crops they grew (which included cotton from which they wove clothing), these people gathered wild plants for food and for the raw materials from which they wove baskets, mats and sandals. They hunted small game and they kept dogs as pets. They kept eagles and turkeys, too, as a source of feathers for ritual purposes and for decoration. Their clay pottery cooking and storage vessels were well made and distinctively decorated. Except in the driest years these people produced more than they needed for survival, and they were visited by traders from whom they obtained such exotic luxuries as gaudy parrot feathers and small handmade copper bells.

They were rich.

Their cities were surely the most important, though indirect, source of their wealth. Carefully, often beautifully built of salmon pink, brick red and caramel-colored stone in protected places within the canyons through which the water flowed to nurture their crops, the cities were densely populated and isolated from one another despite the cultural connections which linked them. Within them grew an intricate set of social conventions, based on religious understandings and kinship, including communal patterns of work sharing. The productiveness of their life ways made of these people an easy going, hard working, rather optimistic folk, unaggressive and generally incurious.

Their success did not last; not in the full flower of its widest development at any rate. Archeologists are not in complete agreement about the factors which forced change upon this prosperous people, though they do tend to agree that these changes began to occur in the middle of the 15th century. It may have been that the delicate balance of climate shifted almost imperceptibly toward aridity, gradually exhausting all but the most dependable sources of water and forcing the abandonment of fields and of the great cities which were dependent on them. There is some evidence, not yet developed conclusively, that the people in some of the cities constructed canals at about this time, a suggestion which lends weight to the theory that something had happened to affect their water sources. Some archeologists are persuaded that the very size and complexity of the cities prompted their abandonment, that social pressures created factions within them and that internal squabbling, intensified, perhaps, by the steadily increasing press of population, and the dwindling water supplies, led to the abandonment of many of the cities. It may have been both of these things simultaneously and other factors not yet deduced from the hollow remains of the silent, brooding sculpture palaces that stare out over the weedy ground that once sprouted corn and beans and squash and cotton.

It was also the arrival of the Diné.

No one can say with any certainty when the Diné crossed to the south shore of the San Juan River, bedevilled by the Utes behind them, to enter the Pueblo country. Some informed guesses range back to a thousand years ago, though the earliest definite physical evidence of their presence dates back only half that time. Whenever it was that they came, they made their presence quickly felt.

The Diné were a rude and violent people, nothing like the sophisticated farmers whose domain they infiltrated. They could grub crops after a fashion, and they could hunt, but they had no more wealth than they could carry, and their command over the spiritual forces of the world was puny and weak. The riches of the Pueblo communities over-awed them, excited their envy, and dared their cunning and courage. The Diné were fighters.

And for all their crudeness they were a good deal more than the hooligans that the comparison with the ancestral Pueblo peoples suggests. For fifteen generations they had been moving south from the British Columbia forests in which the Athabascan language speaking peoples are centered. So long a time among enemies—and anyone not a Diné was an enemy—had made them more adaptable than most peoples, and had taught them an appreciation of the benefits of foreign ways. During their long migration they had borrowed from their neighbors, stolen from them and married with them, and had become in the process an extremely heterogeneous people physically and highly receptive culturally. They scattered out through the unpopulated lands between the pueblo cities, and where there was a trace of water and a patch of fertile ground they settled in families and small groups.

At first they concentrated in the canyons and washes spilling north into the valley of the San Juan River; as time passed they pressed farther to the south and east, deeper into what is now New Mexico. This gradual encroachment occupied several hundred years, and while there were countless scuffles and clashes with the Pueblos, it was not a violent invasion as we tend to think of it today. Rather it was similar to erosion, with long periods of seeming calm and only the barest perceptible movement, punctuated by occasional moments of dramatic activity. Sporadically the Diné attacked Pueblo cities, killing and driving away the men, taking the women and children as captives (and ultimately assimilating them; the traditions of the modern descendants of the Diné indicate that twenty of the tribal clans originated with women who were not themselves Diné) and looting the material wealth. But these local occasions of violence occurred within long

periods of general calm, and even if it had occurred to the unwarlike Pueblos to mount a concerted resistance against the interlopers, their isolation from one another (as much a matter of attitude as of physical distance) prevented it. Thus by trading and raiding the Diné acquired many of the elements that had made the pueblo civilization so strikingly successful. They obtained corn and the techniques for cultivating it—including the proper chants and rituals by which to encourage the cooperation of the forces at work in the wind and the rain.

The Pueblos, meanwhile, were faring badly. The complex and interacting causes of change affecting them had forced the abandonment of many of their smaller cities in favor of a general movement to the south and east into larger and more densely populated communities, especially along the Rio Grande of New Mexico. By the middle of the sixteenth century the number of Pueblo cities had been reduced from several hundred to about seventy, and it was then that the forces for change accelerated beyond all capacity of the Pueblos to contain them. The first harbinger of this new era was the Coronado expedition of 1540.

Coronado came for gold and glory and got neither. Where he had expected the same gilded cities and the accumulated wealth of centuries that Cortez had found in Mexico, and as he knew European cities to be, Coronado found in Cibola only the Pueblo cities of stone and daub, inhabited by a people so stupid and insular that they had no gold of their own whatsoever and only the vaguest inklings of where it might be found. From his headquarters in the conquered Zuñi pueblo of Hawikuh, Coronado sent a small force westward out of New Mexico to explore Tusayan, the seven Hopi pueblos of Arizona.

There the Spaniards were met with a line drawn across their path with colored meal, the traditional "no trespassing" sign of the Hopis. The Spaniards scattered the meal in the wind as they ran on the attack, and the Hopi resistance was broken after a brief skirmish in which a number of their fighters were killed. After receiving gifts of turquoise and food from the seven cities, and informing their populations that they now had obligations of loyalty to the Spanish Crown and obedience to the Christian Church, the Spaniards departed. With them they carried word of an immense chasm farther to the west through which a great river flowed, and from the Zuñi pueblos Coronado sent an exploring party to find it. Thus did the Grand Canyon come under the white man's gaze for the first time; of the Diné Coronado and his choniclers left no mention.

Despite their new status as a part of the Spanish Empire the Hopi were left fairly well to their own devices for many years. The Spanish efforts at establishing themselves in this new region were concentrated in the Rio Grande Valley of New Mexico far to the east of the Hopi country, and far to the south and west in the low desert country of the Yumas, Pimas and Papagos. Yet news reached the Hopis of the effect of the Spanish presence on these distant peoples, and when a prospecting party left a pair of priests among them in 1581, the Hopi poisoned them.

Two years later another party came in search of the missing priests, and managed to make an amiable visit in spite of discovering their deaths. The Hopi had apparently learned something about how to deal with the Spaniards without bloodshed by this time, for they allowed themselves to be persuaded to reveal the location of ore deposits far to the west. The Spaniards departed at once—and actually did find outcroppings which bore evidence of crude workings, presumably the ore bodies of present-day Jerome overlooking the Verde Valley.

In 1598 the Spanish tide inundated New Mexico in earnest. Juan de Oñate, son of the discoverer of the Zacatecas silver bonanza, was given command of a force of soldiers, missionaries and colonists to settle the Rio Grande Valley. And while the Hopis escaped the direct effect of Spanish occupation, they were considered "pacified" by the Spaniards, and their cities used as convenient resting and provisioning places in the relentless search for gold and silver.

Of the Diné the Spaniards had nothing to say until well into the seventeenth century despite the fact that their greatest concentration was in northeastern New Mexico, much closer to the Spanish colonizing effort than the Hopi pueblos. In 1626 a Spanish priest noted the existence of a people he called *Apaches de Navaju*, a corruption of the Tewa Pueblo words meaning "enemies with the cultivated fields". He identified two relatively cohesive groups of these people, both of them living in New Mexico to the east and northeast of the pueblo of Jemez.

As quickly as they could organize the effort, the Spaniards sent missionaries to the Diné, or the Navajos as the Spaniards called them. The Navajos politely sent the priests away. They were not attracted to the prospect of forced labor, whippings and hangings which were the everyday accompaniment of Christianity in the pueblos.

At the same time the Spaniards made a number of unsuccessful attempts to establish priests in the Hopi pueblos. They managed it at last on the eve of the great Pueblo Uprising of 1680.

In the one hundred forty years since the arrival of Coronado, the Pueblos had experienced the changing fortress strongholds of their traditions into prisons. From the priests they had received peach trees from Spain, sheep and beatings for the practice of their old religion. For the soldiers they were required to care for horses, but the penalty for riding one was death. Public whippings were lavished on religious leaders who were discovered practicing the old ways, and some were hanged for it. So oppressive and foreign were the Spaniards that for the first time the pueblo peoples of New Mexico and Arizona united in a concerted action. On a given day in 1680 they burst out simultaneously in open rebellion against the Spaniards. Priests and settlers were slaughtered, and the Spanish soldiers chased south in a rout. The Spanish missions, including the one at Awatavi in the Hopi country of Arizona, were pulled down and the old religion resumed.

But no sooner were the pueblos freed of Spanish tyranny than they began to suffer from the violent depredations of the Navajos, Utes and Comanches whom the Spanish military presence had held in check. As early as 1672 a party of Navajos had swept eastward out of the desert to pour over the Zuñi pueblo of Hawikuh, looting and destroying the settlement with far less restraint than Coronado had shown more than a century before. Now raids from the east and the north were launched against the pueblos as well. Sheep were stolen by the thousands and herded beyond the reach of pueblo retaliation; but while the Utes and Comanches were content to slaughter their stolen animals for food, the Navajos borrowed yet another technique from the pueblo people and husbanded their booty. Thus they assured themselves a constant source of both wool and meat—wealth, in fact—and in the process changed their life ways dramatically, becoming a pastoral people as well as cultivators of the soil.

The Navajos bore no malice against the Hopis, Zuñis or the other Pueblo people on whom they now preyed with abandon. But it was not their way to accumulate wealth slowly, through the cultivation of their crops. In their tradition the method of getting wealth was to take it from someone else, and the pueblo-dwellers, no matter how exemplary their spiritual and material ways, were not, after all, Diné (which means simply "The People" in the Navajo language). The temptation their flocks represented was irresistible.

The Spaniards made three attempts to recapture the pueblos before the Vargas expedition of 1693 was successful. Three years later the pueblos again rebelled, this time unsuccessfully. Many of the pueblo people, in terror and despair at the expectation of Spanish vengeance, fled their ancestral homes forever. Some surrendered themselves for protection to their traditional enemies surrounding them, including the Navajos; others—including a sizeable Tewa community—established themselves with the Hopis where they believed they would be beyond the reach of Spanish retaliation. Hano, on First Mesa in the Hopi reservation of present-day Arizona, is populated by Tewa people whose legends tell of the welcome accorded their ancestors by the Hopis, grateful for more fighters to defend against the Navajo menace.

It was seven years after the reconquest of the New Mexican pueblos before the Spaniards could spare the energy to re-establish their mission at Awatavi. And when the people there began to demonstrate a sympathy toward the presence of the priests and a willingness to co-operate with them, their neighbors on the other Hopi mesas suddenly attacked the city, destroyed it, massacred its inhabitants and put the priests to death. The Hopi incuriosity toward foreign ways had become revulsion and stiffened into active resistance against them. It is this attitude which has permitted them perhaps the greatest determination and success in preserving their traditions against the vast impact of European civilization. Unlike the acquisitive Navajos, the Hopi washed their hands of it.

By the early years of the eighteenth century their raiding had brought the Navajos strongly to the Spanish attention, and they received the customary Spanish overtures delivered by troops and priests. Missions were authorized and two of them established by the middle of the eighteenth century. Despite the success of the padres at Cebolleta in inducing some five hundred Navajos to settle there, they generally ignored the missionary effort. As a consequence of their avoidance of the Spaniards, and of the Utes whom they hated and feared even more (and who were as busy raiding as the Navajos themselves), the center of the Navajo country began to shift progressively farther to the west and south. By 1780, when some of the people were driving Spanish colonists out of their lands in the Cebolleta Mountains of New Mexico, other Navajos had settled as far west as the Canyon de Chelly in Arizona.

These Navajos were now quite a different people than the rough savages who had crossed the San Juan River so many years before. They had become spiritually and materially prosperous as herdsmen, farmers and weavers, and the horses and weapons they had gathered over generations of raiding had made them the supreme fighting force in the region between the Rio Grande Valley of New Mexico and the Hopi Mesas of Arizona. Yet despite their long history of violent confrontations with their neighbors they were not a military people; their fighting was either retaliatory or piratical in nature, aimed at either vengeance or booty. Their independence halted them from becoming soldierly.

The Spaniards mounted a few punitive expeditions against the Navajos—notably the force which succeed in annihilating a band of men, women and children in the Canyon del Muerto in 1804—but for the most part the Spaniards were forced to respond to the Navajo threat simply by strengthening their defenses. Spanish commanders along the Rio Grande received pleas for assistance against the Navajos from the Hopis as late as 1809 but could do nothing. With the Independence of Mexico in 1810, and the consequent military confusion along the former Spanish frontier, the Navajos abandoned all restraint. Well mounted and well armed they became a merciless scourge, plundering settlements and ranchos of livestock almost at will. So mobile were they that they established contact with other Indian peoples as far afield as the Pawnee of western Nebraska.

In 1846 the American Army of the West came on horseback and afoot to take the field in the war against Mexico. When the Mexican forces abandoned Santa Fe without resistance the Americans occupied and garrisoned the Rio Grande Valley and called for deputations from the Indian tribes in the region. The Pueblo peoples of New Mexico sent representatives, as did even the warlike Apaches who had been as violent in the south as the Navajos had been to the north. The Navajos, however, did not go to the council table. Instead they formed a raiding party to attack one of the New Mexico pueblos, kill half a dozen men, capture the women and children and drive away hundreds of sheep, cattle, horses and mules.

At once, to the joy and relief of the beleaguered New Mexicans, the American commander sent three detachments of Missouri Volunteers west into the Navajo country. One of them managed to make contact with Narbona, a leading man among the Navajos of New Mexico, who promised to meet with the American commander in an effort to arrive at a formula for peace. On their return to Cebolleta, however, the soldiers discovered that in their absence their horses had been stolen by Navajo raiders. When the peace conference was actually held, a dispute over a stolen horse resulted in the

shooting of the 80 year old Narbona and the flight of the rest of the Navajos. Between 1846 and 1850 the Navajos stole an estimated 800,000 sheep and cattle and 20,000 horses, most of them from New Mexico.

In 1852 the Americans built Fort Defiance in a green meadow in Arizona's high mesa country near the border with New Mexico. They garrisoned it heavily and provided a succession of Indian Agents. For a few years there was a relative and tentative calm, thanks in large measure to the effectiveness of Captain Henry Dodge who, as Indian Agent, won the respect and co-operation of the Navajos. With his death, however, conditions degenerated rapidly. They fell apart completely when the Army commander at Fort Defiance ordered sixty Navajo horses shot for grazing on the meadow adjacent to the fort. In his view it was a matter of discipline; to the Navajos it was an atrocity. Horses were wealth, and at the same time they were the means by which to acquire more wealth. Stealing horses—that the Navajos understood; but to slaughter them wantonly was obscene and unforgivable. Incidents between the soliders and the Navajos pyramided, culminating at last with an attack on Fort Defiance itself. The attack was a disaster, and Navajo fighting men scattered into the deepest and least accessible corners of the Navajo country to take refuge. Shortly afterward, to their utter amazement, the soldiers marched out of Fort Defiance and left the Navajo country altogether.

The Navajos' satisfaction at this unexpected turn of events was short-lived. With the departure of the soldiers the Utes and Hopis and the vengeful New Mexicans became aggressively hostile, and the area became a bloody four-cornered free-for-all. The Navajos plundered ranchos and settlements almost within sight of Santa Fe itself, and in turn were captured and bartered as slaves. As many as 5,000 Navajos were thought to have been kept as slaves at this time by other tribes, by Mexicans and by New Mexicans of every race.

It had been the urgent necessity for troops on the battlefields of the Civil War and not the ineffectual Navajo attack which had prompted the federal abandonment of Fort Defiance; after a brief Confederate occupation of the Rio Grande Valley Union troops were soon in control of New Mexico and Arizona again. These troops launched a campaign against the belligerent Mescalero Apaches and brought them into a reservation established at Fort Sumner in eastern New Mexico. The Army then turned its attention to the Navajos; Kit Carson was called out of retirement to lead the fight against them.

In the deep winter of early 1864 he set out with a force of fewer than 400 men, striking directly into the deepest heart of the Navajo homeland: the incomparably beautiful Canyon de Chelly. As he went he destroyed crops, gathered up sheep and horses, and took captive the few Navajos who strayed incautiously out of hiding. During one seven day period his soldiers were employed continuously at burning vast tracts of corn and wheat and chopping down the peach trees the Navajos had long ago obtained from the Pueblo people. When he had made his sweep he called for the Navajo surrender and returned to Fort Defiance. The expedition had resulted in only 23 Navajos killed, 34 captured and about 200 surrendered voluntarily, but the devastation of the Navajo crops meant, simply, starvation. And more than that: Carson's uncontested invasion of the hitherto inviolable Canyon de Chelly made further resistance seem fruitless to the Navajos. They began to surrender. By March, 2400 of them were camped under guard at Fort Defiance, and more groups were surrendering daily.

From Fort Defiance they began the 300 mile Long Walk to Fort Sumner and the farmlands set aside for them at the Bosque Redondo, a cottonwood grove at the edge of the Pecos River.

They walked out of the tumbled land which their legends and myths had assured them was made expressly for their use, into a flat region without horizons in which their gods were not at home and their rituals ineffective. Kit Carson had defeated them; the Long Walk beat them hollow.

Their crops alongside the Pecos did not prosper. The first year they nourished a plague of grasshoppers; drought and wind destroyed them in the years after that. The Army, unexpectedly, was required to feed them—with food they found unpalatable— and the 400-man garrison at Fort Sumner went on half rations to do it. The Indian Commissioners diverted almost three-fourths of the $100,000 provided to feed, clothe and outfit the Navajos into their own pockets. Comanches stole the Navajo horses and cattle, and Mexicans stole the women and children. In the face of this continuing disaster the Navajos refused to plant at all in 1867, and the least demoralized of them began slipping away from the reservation. In June, 1868, the government received the eager promises of the Navajos never to fight again, and sent them home.

They have kept their promise. In the years since their return to the high mesa country of Arizona and the adjacent parts of New Mexico and Utah they have become the most numerous Indian tribe in the United States. Yet their difficulties have not ended.

Of the approximately 15,000,000 acres of the present Navajo reservation, about twelve per cent is wasteland. Two-thirds of the reservation is so marginally productive of forage that a single sheep requires from 17 to 50 acres of it to graze. In addition, a drought cycle which began in the 1880s and which has been intensified in its effect by severe overgrazing by Navajo sheep bands since the turn of the century, has resulted in the loss on nearly half the Navajo land of as much as twenty-five per cent of the topsoil, and of as much as seventy-five per cent from another three and a half million acres. By 1945 the productive capacity of the Navajo land had been reduced to about half of what it had been in 1868, while the population it was required to aid had increased several times.

With the emergence in the 1940s of the Navajo tribal council as a real focus of the tribe's energies and ambitions, and a growing willingness among the Navajos to act in concert rather than making their decisions as small groups and families, programs have been developed which benefit the tribe as a whole. But that kind of co-operation does not come easily to a people whose traditions do not include a broad and embracing political experience, and the going is slow. As rich as they are in so many ways of their own, they are cash poor, and to be cash poor in the white man's United States is a disaster. Still, the history of the Navajos over the past four hundred years is a chronicle of successful adaptation to one revolutionary change after another, and there is little doubt that they will find the means with which to meet what may be the most difficult and pervasive challenge they have ever faced.

The Hopi attitude toward American influence is much the same as it was toward the Spanish: general disinclination, reluctant compliance when necessary, and occasional active resistance. Their reservation is completely enclosed within that of the Navajos, and life in their mesa-top cities proceeds much as it did a century ago. Protestant missionaries have made better progress than the Spanish Catholics did, and many Hopis have adopted at least some of the trappings of our contemporary civilization. But the essential ingredients of Hopi life within their cities remains largely unaffected by the American world surrounding them. Oraibi, the Hopi city at the top of Third Mesa, was established in the waning years of the thirteenth century, and usually is acknowledged as the oldest continuously occupied settlement within the boundaries of the United States. This in itself is testimony to the conservative nature of the Hopi character and to the enduring satisfactions which the Hopi ways provide.

[THE MOUNTAIN FORESTS]

The Arizona desert takes hold of a man's mind and shakes it. And because the forest only strokes gently at his memory, the mind's eye often overlooks it. Yet the forests of Arizona are more extensive than those of Maine and Wisconsin and nearly as large as the Michigan woods. More than twenty-five per cent of Arizona landscapes are forested; some twenty million acres of wooded lands representing priceless resources of recreation, timber, grazing, jobs and, most precious of all in this arid land, water.

At the edge of the Plateau Province of northeastern Arizona high grasslands slope away to the south and southwest, ending abruptly at the Mogollon Rim, a cliff of from a few hundred to fifteen hundred feet high. At its eastern end the White Mountains, huge mountains of ancient lava, are heaped up, dome upon dome, to an elevation of nearly twelve thousand feet above the level of the sea, and at many places in the west, where the Rim is lower and less pronounced, the cliff is obscured by relatively recent lava flows. At the base of the Rim the landscape is mountainous; some thirty distinct steepsided ranges crowd together there, separated by deep narrow valleys in a belt from ten to one hundred fifty miles wide. It is on this rumpled band of mountains at the base of the Mogollon Rim that Arizona's forests are centered: a broad, brush-stroke of green beginning at the New Mexico border in the White Mountains and curving about two hundred fifty miles northwestward as far as the San Francisco volcanic field near Flagstaff and Williams. There the brush was lifted from the canvas to splash forest green across the Kaibab Plateau on the north rim of the Grand Canyon, drip it on the Defiance Uplift in the high mesa country of Arizona's northeast corner and on the mountains around Prescott, and then to spatter the summits of the Cerbat and Hualapai Ranges in northwestern Arizona and the Santa Ritas, the Santa Catalinas, the Chiricahuas, the Dragoons and other mountain ranges of the southeast.

Most of this inland sea of green is pine forest, giving way at its high elevations to fir and spruce, and at its lower edges to broad foothill fringes tufted with pinyon and juniper. There is marvelous variety to Arizona's forests, but it is the green-grizzled ponderosa pine, comprising the longest unbroken stand of them in any state in the union, that gives the wild pagan cathedral of Arizona's highland forests their character.

Mountains rise up to pierce through the blanketing forest in only two places in Arizona: at the sharp summits of the San Francisco Peaks and at the bulbous eminence of Baldy Peak in the White Mountains. There, in the topmost pinnacles above timberline, only a few hardy grasses and groundhugging shrubs survive the freezing temperatures of winter, the nine month burden of the snow pack and the ceaseless whipping of the winds. Such plants as do survive are bunched in unexpected ways away from their cousins in sheltered places and sometimes develop on other summits and in the Arctic lowlands.

Lichen stains the slabbed expanses of stone with red and green, brown and gold and black, but the soils resulting from their microscopic nibblings are mostly swept away by the winds or washed downslope by the melting snows. Only pinches of it lodge in crevices, and only there, where there is a mite of soil, can seeds sprout and root themselves in a precarious balance between too little exposure to the sun and too much exposure to the wind. The animal life is as limited. Ermine weasels dart about among the rocks, and mountain sheep spent summers here before they were hunted out. Golden eagles thump their heavy wings against the thin air to heave themselves into soaring flight.

Downslope some two thousand feet from the summit of the San Francisco Peaks the naked stone is wrapped around by the collar of the flowing forest cape that trails out east into New Mexico: a frayed and threadbare collar of gnarled and stunted trees. They are Engelmann spruce and bristlecone pine, tormented victims of the winds and frosts, some of them so savaged by the elements that they lie flat against the earth.

Farther down the mountainside the spruce grow full and strong, but the bristlecone pine grow only here at timberline and in a few scattered groves downslope where conditions approximate those at the heights. Ice-grained winter winds have scoured them of bark and twisted their burly trunks like hawsers. Their frayed and brambled limbs, upstretched in tattered homage to the sun, have been foreshortened by centuries of too-brief summers. Their roots press with sullen desperation into the shivered stone, and by the looks of them they have only the most tenuous grip on life. Yet the bristlecone pine is the oldest living thing on earth.

Not the trees growing at timberline in the San Francisco Peaks; these are relative babies, seeds that took root during the reign of Sven Forked-Beard in Denmark and Ethelred the Unready in England a thousand years ago. It is in the White Mountains straddling the Nevada-California border that the oldest specimens of bristlecone pine have been discovered. There the patriarch trees that took root in the time of Abraham are still flourishing, four times and more the age of the Arizona trees, and more than a thousand years older than the oldest known sequoia.

Rarely do bristlecones grow to a height of more than forty feet, and their average is scarcely half that. The combination of small size, small numbers, slow growth, contorted shape and inaccessibility has exempted them from commercial use. Forest scientists have quite enough on their plates already with the immense and immediate problems posed by more common forest trees to devote much more than a passing glance of curiosity at the bristlecone as yet. The bristlecone pine is extremely useful in extending back to limits of tree-ring dating, but so far there are only theories to explain the tree's remarkable longevity. One of them suggests that the relatively high resin content is the key to survival. Another proposes that the relatively small stands of bristlecone pine on the western mountain summits are only the remnants of whole forests that flourished during the colder climates accompanying the Ice Ages. But other trees and plant life found at or near timberline in the San Francisco Mountains are also found in profusion in more northerly latitudes and the bristlecone pine is not.

Timberline does not collar the mountain evenly around; it is higher on the back of the neck, on the south and the west, where the sun's rays strike the mountainside during the heat of the day, and lower in the east where sunlight strikes early and briefly. On the north slopes it is lower still; there the sunlight touches the mountain only a little below sunset if it touches at all. Thus on the San Francisco Mountains timberline occurs at about 10,700 feet on the northeast slope and at about 11,500 on the southwest. Below timberline the forest sweeps away in every direction, a province of dims and deeps and vast expanse like a sea. And like a sea the forest is never still, always in the grip of imperceptible motion.

The bristlecone pine thin out and vanish immediately below timberline. The Engelmann spruce straighten up to become full bodied, robust trees, growing in dense stands as low as 8,500 on the northeast slope of the mountain and to about 9,200 on the southwest. They are large trees, reaching up eighty feet and more, with trunks three feet in diameter and spreading branches that droop slightly toward the ground as they taper toward the conical crown of the tree. Corkbark fir, a close cousin distinguished by a thin layer of smooth, spongy bark, is a near neighbor in the high forest; in the White Mountains the mature corkbark firs are among the largest in the world.

Douglas fir rise up to mingle in the lower reaches of the Engelmann spruce belt. The Douglas fir is the largest tree native to Arizona, growing at maturity to heights of from 100 to 150 feet and occasionally approaching 200 feet. The crown of the tree is open and broadly conical, the trunk from three to six feet in diameter at the base, and the branches, dripping with blue-green needles, sag gently below the horizontal. It is the most important timber tree in the United States, though in Arizona it accounts for only a small percentage of the commercial harvest because it grows only in the heights above the far larger and more accessible ponderosa pine forests. Limber pine and white fir are commonly found in the forest belt dominated by the Douglas fir. As recently as twenty years ago the white fir was considered a weed tree by loggers who are now glad to harvest them as timber. On the San Francisco Peaks the Douglas fir forest descends to about 7,200 feet on the north and east exposures and to about 8,200 feet on the south and west.

These forest belts can be more clearly marked out here, on paper, than on the mountainsides. There they blend almost imperceptibly into one another, influenced by a variety of elements including quite local climatic conditions–microclimates, they are called—which often lead to pronounced contradictions to the general rules. Because they intermix, and because of the economics of forest management and timber harvest, the forest from timberline to the lower limits of the Douglas fir is considered as a unit in Arizona. Eight trees occur in this forest, seven of them conifers. A ninth tree, the Gambel oak, is also found in the high forests, but since it seldom occurs as a part of the forest's crown canopy it is considered a shrub by foresters. The enveloping cloak of the mixed conifer forest is patched here and there by thick stands of aspen, their white trunks like the slender legs of schoolgirls, their bright, trembling leaves a vivacious contrast to the grave and moody expanse of conifers.

With the sudden increase in lumber requirements during World War II there was relatively little logging done in Arizona's mixed conifer forest, and consequently little empirical data has been gathered concerning the specific management requirements of the region. What active forest management has been attempted in the past was largely directed toward timber production. And while increasing demand has made these forests of the mountain highlands an ever more desirable source of timber, other considerations are also emerging. Water yield, recreation, livestock grazing—all these uses of the forest prompt the adoption of logging techniques which may be less productive when measured in board feet of timber alone, but which are compatible with the concept of multiple use to which the forests are committed.

In Arizona many of these techniques were pioneered in the great ponderosa pine forests that occupy the next stratum of elevation below the mixed conifer belt. On San Francisco Mountain the upper limits of the ponderosa pine are at about 7,200 feet on the north and east exposures, and at about 8,200 feet on the south and west.

The ponderosa pine is second only to the Douglas fir in total stand among all tree species in the United States and is a characteristic forest tree in every western state. In Arizona it is found in the higher elevations of every section of the state except the central and southwestern, and in the mountains of the southeast corner of the state it shares the summits with Apache pine and Chihuahua pine.

The ponderosa pine commonly grows to heights of from eighty to 125 feet in Arizona, only occasionally reaching 150 feet. It matures at about 250 years and survives at maturity for another 250, though the Arizona trees are somewhat shorter-lived than those of the Pacific northwest. Rare specimens have been found which can be dated back a thousand years by tree ring count, but none of them in Arizona.

In appearance the ponderosa pine is a little like the Arizona frontiersman: tall and straight but a little raggedy at the elbows and faring best when separated somewhat from its nearest neighbor. Like the Arizona pioneer —and unlike most commercially valuable conifers—the ponderosa pine can tolerate relatively high temperatures and relatively low amounts of precipitation. As a result it is the lowest growing of all Arizona timber trees, extending down to about 6,000 feet on the north and east slopes of the San Francisco Peaks and to about 7,000 feet in more sun-exposed locations.

The ponderosa pine has both a vertical tap root and a well-developed and uniform horizontal branch root system. This is one of the critical factors in fostering growth in hot, dry locations, for it permits the efficient absorption of ground moisture when it is available in the soil, yet prevents sucking the soil rapidly dry when it is scarce. In seasons of drought the ponderosa pine can drastically curtail its transpiration rate so that moisture gathered in at the roots is not given off at the needles but held longer in the tree.

Yet the ponderosa pine is classified as an intolerant species; that is, it requires certain quite specific conditions in which to prosper. For example, seedlings must have at least fifty per cent shade, but less than sixty-seven per cent. If they receive more than fifty per cent sunlight they cannot withstand the crushing weight of the winter snowpack to which they are also exposed. It presses their limber, fingerling trunks flat against the earth winter after winter, maiming them until they succumb. More than sixty-seven per cent shade and they grow runty if they grow at all, and usually die within a decade of taking root. Other elements, too, affect the seedling's prospects for healthy development: rainfall within certain limits at the proper season, temperatures, soil conditions and the depredations of wildlife and grazing cattle.

Soil conditions play a more important part in forest life than is generally recognized, especially at lower elevations where temperatures are higher and ground moisture evaporation becomes an increasingly critical factor. Where soils are heavy, as those with a high clay content, trees are usually spaced wider apart because moisture is not readily absorbed for retention, and because root penetration by seedlings is more difficult. Where heavy soils occur in combination with other unfavorable conditions the forest trees may be unable to establish themselves at all. Thus a mountain meadow, enclosed by dense forest, lush with grasses but bare of trees, or a grove of a "foreign" species like an island in a sea of dominant trees. Where there are sandy or graveled soils ponderosa pine will flourish as low as 5,500 feet, for the seedling roots can penetrate as easily as the percolating moisture. Even a relatively infertile soil can be beneficial to the young trees in critical locations by preventing the establishment of competing plant life.

Explorers who left behind them the earliest written descriptions of the ponderosa pine forests of Arizona consistently mention their open character. The honey brown carpet of needles pierced by grasses and the absence of underbrush prompted many to compare the virgin forests to carefully tended parks.

The loggers came late to the Arizona forests. There was a small saw-pit in operation in the Santa Rita Range near Tucson in the mid-1850s and a steam powered sawmill on Granite Creek near Prescott ten years later. These early operations were small because the demand for lumber was small in the frontier villages of Arizona and bad roads and the lack of adequate transportation isolated the Arizona forests from the major lumber markets. Thus it was only where underground mining required prodigious quan-

tities of timber that the forests were stripped bare, and then only in the years before the creation of the Forest Reserves in the last decade of the 19th century. A survey undertaken in 1925 revealed that nine-tenths of Arizona's original forested lands were still tree-covered in that year, and that fully a fourth of the original forests remained untouched in virgin timber.

Logging techniques have changed enormously, even since 1925. Technological change has played a part, as it has in all of man's endeavors, but changes in philosophy have been even more important. In the bad old days the single motive in a logger's heart was to cut timber, and the more the better. The easier and faster the better, too, which meant clearcutting whole tracts of mountainside and dragging out the logs without concern for the smaller trees which were inevitably crushed and mangled, or the landscape deeply scarred by the ensuing erosion. In those days the timber cut could be so concentrated that permanent logging camps could be established. Maverick and Happy Jack are two of the best-known and longest-lived of the logging camps in Arizona.

But Maverick is closed now, and Happy Jack may be living on borrowed time. With forest management policies becoming more complex and intensified the logging companies can no longer concentrate their crews as they once did. Lighter cuts are being made over greater areas. Loggers now thin stands of pine the way a farmer thins carrots, and growing timber bigger and faster as a result. Cuts are confined to old trees and to sick ones, and mature trees are left standing along the roadsides for the pleasure they give there.

Already the old-time logger is only a memory. He was the fellow wearing a shirt "half an inch thick and so scratchy the ordinary human beings began to itch the minute they got into the same room with it" and "corks" in his boots, spikes that allowed him to "set his heel down in the pine floor, twist his foot dexterously, and rip out an entire board without batting an eye" in the course of a spree after months of isolation in the woods. Now the loggers commute to the forest from pleasant homes and families.

With few exceptions the four million acres of commercial forest in Arizona exist above 5,500 feet in elevation. Below 5,500 feet the precipitation is too light and soil moisture evaporation takes place too rapidly to support even the hardy ponderosa pine. The foothills at this altitude, and as high as 7,000 feet in places—notably in the high mesa country in the northeast—are the domain of the pinyons and junipers.

The juniper is a stiff-limbed, shaggy, lop-

sided tree and the pinyon pine is a sap-drooling potbellied runt. Compared with the trees in the forests above them they are good-for-nothings. They grow scattered across the landscape like tufts in a bedspread, and they cover some fifteen million acres in Arizona, about a fifth of the total west of the Rockies. Because no commercial uses have yet been developed for these trees, the use of the extensive pinyon-juniper woodlands in Arizona at present is confined almost exclusively to wildlife habitat and livestock grazing.

Arizona's grazing lands descend deeper into the lowlands than the pinyon and juniper trees can venture, into the chapparal: the brush forest.

Chaparral is a dry, sinewy, unpalatable salad of some fifty different plant species that only occasionally grow to the height of a man's belt. They are all broad-leaved evergreens, usually dominated by one or more varieties of scrub oak. And for all its lack of grandeur, the chaparral can be almost as impenetrable as a tropical rain forest to a man on foot. In Arizona the chaparral occurs from about six thousand feet in elevation to about four thousand feet and spreads across some five million acres in the lower foothills.

Below the chaparral horizon is the desert. Where soils are basalt the ground cover tends to be grass; where it is sedimentary it is most often the narrowleafed shrubwoods of the desert: palo verde, mesquite, ironwood and the like. Saguaros march splendidly up the hillsides to meet the chaparral, and other, smaller cactuses mingle in its lower edges.

Arizona's forests have fostered whole industries of livestock and lumber, and now recreation is emerging as an increasingly important forest industry as the southwest becomes increasingly populated and the populations of other regions become increasingly mobile. Seven National Forests embracing eleven million acres are contained within Arizona's boundaries.

The state's highland forests stand in serene contradiction to the stereotyped picture of Arizona as a badland of sandy barrens dappled with spiny cactus and otherworldly shrub-trees, an outlandish garden of fierce vegetables baking in the oven of a desert noon. Nothing could be more appropriate, for no state is so distinguished by extravagant contradictions as Arizona.

[TWO MARVELS]

They call the Salt the river that came to town and stayed. It snakes down out of the White Mountain high country to the northeast, hesitates and grows plump behind a series of storage dams, thins down and braids out into a system of canals—and vanishes.

When traffic is light you can hear it gurgling beneath the streets of Phoenix. In the pleated fields that surround the city you can see the sun glinting off shallow parallel rows of it. But only rarely does the Salt ever reappear in its broad, sandy channel below the city to trickle on toward the Gila, the Colorado and the sea. The Salt River is just plain used up in Phoenix.

So ingeniously and efficiently are the waters of the Salt employed, in fact, that a quarter million acres of central Arizona desert have been transformed into one of the most fertile and productive agricultural areas in the world, and in its center has risen one of the major cities of the West. Where only saguaros and scrubby desert vegetation had maintained a precarious hold on life before, now cash crops valued at some fifty million dollars are harvested annually, and cattle herds worth twenty million dollars thrive. Electricity generated at the hydroelectric dams on the Salt serves the rapidly growing Phoenix Metropolitan Area, vast tracts of two adjoining counties, several of the state's largest mines and smelters, and is exported during periods of reduced local demand as far away as the Pacific northwest.

As a direct result of putting the Salt to work there are presently more people living within the Phoenix city limits than in the entire state of Nevada. More than that: it is said that, harnessed, the Salt River is the foundation of all permanent wealth in Central Arizona.

The genius who conceived of systematically irrigating the broad valley floor and devised the canal system by which to accomplish it is unknown. He was one of the people we call the Hohokam, the prehistoric master farmers of Arizona's southern desert lowlands. They were a people of varied and vigorous culture, but they had no written language and had ceased to exist as a people by the time of the Spanish arrival. Still, archaeologists are persuaded that the Hohokam may have begun developing irrigation canals in the Salt River Valley as early as 500 A.D., improving and extending them until their dispersal in about 1400. Working in large construction gangs with tools of stone and wood the Hohokam had managed to build and maintain more than 125 miles of irrigation canals to carry the waters of the Salt to their corn and cotton fields. One Hohokam city, called Los Muertos by archaeologists, was a thriving community of several hundred persons whose crops were watered by a canal that meandered through six miles of harsh desert landscape from the bank of the Salt.

The causes of the decline and dispersal of the Hohokam are not clearly understood, though it seems likely they were affected by at least some of the changes that brought an end to the great days of the Anasazi in the redrock canyonlands farther north. The generally accepted supposition is that the modern day Pima and Papago people of southern Arizona and northern Sonora are descendants of the ancient Hohokam.

After 1400 the canals they had so laboriously built and the fields they had so painstakingly cleared and tended began to return to the desert: silt filled the canals and scrub brush invaded the cotton and vegetable patches. But for all its ferocity, the desert is a fragile place, and nearly five hundred years after their abandonment scars marking the course of old canals were still faintly visible on the sandy ground.

When Fort McDowell was established to protect early Arizona settlers against Apache raiders at the close of the Civil War, a midwestern farmer named Smith took up some acreage in the Salt River Valley where wild hay grew in abundance, nourished by underground seepage from the river. Smith took the contract to furnish hay to the cavalry at Fort McDowell and hired an old Arizona hand named Jack Swilling to haul it for him. Swilling, prowling the bottoms between trips to the fort, discovered the remnants of the Hohokam canals. Not only did he instinctively recognize them for what they were, he recognized the implications for the valley.

Swilling went to Wickenburg where men with a little money and men at loose ends had been drawn to the mines. There he chartered a ditch company with about twenty members, and issued shares with a theoretical value of ten thousand dollars although the company's actual assets amounted to something more like $400 worth of tools and supplies. The first attempt to clear a ditch proved fruitless when the men struck bedrock at an elevation above the normal flow of the river. A second attempt was successful, however, and in March, 1868, a few acres of hastily cleared desert was inundated with Salt River water. By fall there were a hundred permanent residents farming along the course of the ditch, and a flour mill was under construction nearby.

Swilling himself did not stay to see the valley prosper. Like the prospector who takes more satisfaction in the search for a strike than in the development of the mine, Swilling moved on in 1875. By that time the flour mill was grinding locally grown grain and two more ditches had transformed thousands more acres of scrub desert into productive farms. So clearly successful were these farms, and so hungry for their produce were the isolated settlements of the Arizona frontier that new ditch companies were organized almost as quickly as the legal papers could be drawn up and stock issued. By 1888, the year that archaeologists were gingerly excavating the Hohokam settlement at Los Muertos, eight ditches had been dug and more than one hundred thousand acres were under cultivation.

Water storage facilities along the Salt had been suggested as early as 1876 but no steps had been taken to build them then: the rush to dig new ditches and clear new land had absorbed the energies of the valley's growing population. By the 1880s, though, serious problems had emerged.

One of the most difficult was the matter of water rights, which were based upon prior appropriation. Some of the older ditches tapped the river downstream from the newer ones, and at times of low water long-established farmers suspected that the newcomers upstream were diverting more water to their fields than they were entitled to. Measuring devices were crude and inefficient, and friction began to divide the population of the prosperous valley. The friction was intensified as speculators involved themselves in the water squabbles. Since water rights in the valley represented wealth, they could be pledged as security for loans, and often were. Unredeemed water rights became separated from the lands they irrigated when loans were foreclosed, and their new owners sold or rented the rights to the highest bidder. As a consequence, rich farms were sometimes sold to newcomers who then discovered they had no water with which to irrigate them. Despite the bitterness which led to several killings, most farms were still taking their two crops a year with heartening regularity and prosperity was the rule.

But drought struck in 1897. With little rain in the mountains the Salt dwindled to a trickle. There was little rain in 1898 and 1899, and the Salt River Valley became a miniature dust bowl. Scores of farms were abandoned and at least 75,000 cultivated acres were abandoned back to the desert. Men patrolled the diversion gates with rifles and shotguns to protect their claims to what little moisture still seeped down the channel. Water rights had become a life or death issue and a tangle of law suits was initiated in the courts.

In February, 1900, the rains came at last—but in a single catastrophic mountain storm that sent a flash flood churning down the course of the Salt to destroy every diversion dam along its length. With their mud and earth dams went the farmers' hopes for a spring crop. In March winds came up to sweep the fine topsoil into enormous dust clouds. Hysteria ruled the valley, and despair.

In August a mass meeting was held in the

Dorris Opera House on Phoenix's Central Avenue. At the meeting a committee proposed construction of a water storage dam at Tonto Basin, about eight-five miles northeast of Phoenix and some sixty miles from the nearest railroad. The project would cost from two to five million dollars.

No such amount of money was available in the Territory, and the farmers, speculators and capitalists who were trying to bury their considerable differences in order to make a common effort to acquire it found the going very thorny. But in the spring of 1901 the water in the Salt reached its lowest level in memory, and the committees met with redoubled energy. When at last a plan for constructing and financing the dam was agreed upon, an agent was sent to Washington to ask for federal help with the project.

President McKinley opposed the idea and so did Congress. There was some support, principally from Senator Stewart of Nevada and other representatives of arid western states, but not enough to get the needed help.

Nevertheless, Representative Francis Newlands of Nevada presented a reclamation bill to Congress which would provide the required federal assistance. The new President, Theodore Roosevelt, spoke in favor of federal participation in such projects in his first message to Congress. The Newlands Act passed and became law on June 17, 1902.

Two more years of conciliation was required to reorganize the water users' association to conform with the new federal law, an enormous effort involving not only the energies of the project leaders, but substantial sacrifice from many of the valley's residents. Authorization for the project was at last achieved in June, 1904.

A road was cut along the course of the Salt from the railroad at Mesa for the transportation of materials and equipment to the damsite. A sawmill was built in the Sierra Ancha Mountains to supply more than three million board feet of lumber. Crews of Italian stone masons cut more than 342,000 cubic yards of stone from the hillsides surrounding the site. Construction of the dam itself began in 1905 and was not completed until five years later, more than two years behind schedule and almost fifteen years after the urgent need for it had been recognized in the valley.

Roosevelt Dam is still the largest masonry dam in the world, and it created behind it what was then the world's largest storage reservoir with a capacity of 1,381,580 acre-feet of water. Five 900-kw hydroelectric generators were installed to power pumps which provided water to portions of the valley too high for ordinary ditch irrigation.

Since the 1920s six more dams have been built, four of them on the Salt and two on the Verde, providing an aggregate storage capacity of more than a million and three quarter acre-feet of water and a substantially increased hydroelectric generating capacity. The increasingly intricate system of dams, diversions and 1200 miles of canal delivers an average of a million acre-feet of water to cultivated fields in the Salt River Valley each year, the run-off from nearly thirteen thousand square miles of mountainous country to the north and east. With this water the desert has been made productive to a degree unparalleled in history.

Bounded around by the spiny remains of dead volcanic mountains and grey expanses of desert, the immense man-made oasis of the Salt River Valley with Phoenix rising in its center is a profound achievement. Yet for all its fruitful impact upon the landscape, it seems trivial when compared with a work of nature a few hundred miles to the north at the majestic chasm called Grand Canyon, the greatest natural spectacle on the surface of the earth. In its depths are laid bare rocks laid down more than two billion years ago—half the lifetime of the earth itself.

In that remote age the region through which the canyon cuts today was a warped and buckled mountain range with soaring peaks as high as six or seven miles above the level of the sea. As the nearly imperceptible process of erosion was nibbling at the peaks and prominences of the mighty range, magma, thrust upward from the molten heart of the earth, cooled and solidified as granite deep within them. On the surface of the mountains rivulets scrubbed at the jagged rock and winds rubbed its contours smooth. When millions of years had passed the mountains were reduced to outwashed mudslumps making a rolling plain several thousands square miles in extent with only the stumps of the great ranges protruding slightly above it. And the sea crept in over the surface of the lifeless plain.

There was algae in the sea, perhaps the most advanced form of life on earth at that time, and its remains played a part in the formation of limestone deposits which began to accumulate, mote upon mote, in the seabed. Eons later the seabed was thickly layered with grains of rock and soil washed into the shallow sea by streams and rivers which originated in a faraway mountain range. The shores of the sea slowly advanced and receded, alternately exposing and inundating the ever-increasing accumulations above the eroded mountains.

When more sophisticated forms of plant life had begun to appear in it the sea retreated again and erosion carved the exposed surface.

Later, great fault lines cracked through the crust of the earth to the accompaniment of earthquakes and great blocks of it were tilted slowly upward along these seams to form a new mountain system. Millions more years later—about six hundred million years ago—these mountains, too, had been eroded into a smooth-contoured plain dominated by a few low ridges. Much of the materials deposited so long before at the bottom of the sea were washed away by erosion and the older rock on which the seabed had accumulated for half a billion years was exposed in numerous places. Then the sea returned.

Life in the sea was vastly more varied than it had been before, and in the new seabed gathering in its submerged depths were seaweed and shells as well as the more primitive forms. As the strata thickened at the bottom of the sea, hordes of brachiopods, trilobites and other shellfish were entombed before the land again nudged up above the surface of the sea for a time. When it sank back, lavender limestone formed in the eroded pits and hollows of the uppermost stratum, and these deposits preserved the remains of still more modern creatures of the sea. Again the sea crept away and slithered back. A gray limestone seabed accumulated to a depth of more than five hundred feet before it was once more exposed as dry land to the forces of erosion. Yet again the sea flowed back; its departure this time was extremely slow and reluctant. At its bottom the resulting seabed changed imperceptibly in its thousand-foot thickness from limestone to sandstone formed from the deposits of tidelands and silted river deltas marked by the preserved footprints of amphibians.

When the land had been altogether lifted above the surface of the sea, rivers and streams buried it beneath clay and mud; the remains of ferns and fossil conifers were fossilized within the resulting rock. The climate became progressively drier and hotter; winds swept up soil and heaped it deep over the old stream courses, building dunes that extended from horizon to horizon until they sank beneath the encroaching sea. Movement in the sea depths planed the tops of the dunes, and the centuries overtopped them with limestone before the sea departed. When it returned again another layer of limestone was laid down, and the sea withdrew forever. Three hundred million years had passed since the end of the great mountain building and erosion era which created the bedrock upon which the layered seabeds had been built to a depth of less than a mile.

During the next one hundred fifty million years a thousand feet of wind- and water-borne materials was laid down and eroded away again. Not until about sixty-five million years ago did the cutting of Grand Canyon begin. It was then that the eroded plain, barely above sea level, began to bulge upward in response to forces at work deep within the earth until it had achieved an elevation of about nine thousand feet. The resulting prominence (we now call it the Kaibab Plateau) was lozenge shaped, with its longest dimension running approximately north and south. When it had been formed a river, the product of tributaries from far to the north, ran along its eastern base. This river gathered in the water from the streams and rivulets that began to scar the eastern slope of the young plateau and carried it away southeastward, most probably to empty into the Gulf of Mexico. On the west snow-melt, storm runoff and spring water began to scribe small channels in the sloping side of the plateau; they united at the foot of the plateau to create a second river, this one flowing west and south to merge with other streams and empty eventually into the Gulf of California.

In the course of several million years the streams draining the western side of the plateau had cut deep channels, and as they grew deeper they had clawed like greedy fingers into the exposed limestone, extending progressively farther eastward into the fat rump of the plateau. At the same time, the river draining the east slope of the plateau had been dammed far to the south and east by enormous movements in the earth's crust there, forming a vast inland sea which extended back eventually to the southeastern foot of the plateau. As the river below the eastern edge of the plateau continued to feed the inland sea, the tributaries of the western river continued to gnaw deeper into the soft limestone spine of the plateau and at length one of them pushed its beginnings completely through to the east side of the upthrust land mass. This small channel now connected with the great flow from the north, and captured it. Some of the water on the east side of the plateau continued to feed the inland sea, but ever greater amounts of it were channeled west to join the western river, traveling in a great arc through the gully cut across the back of the plateau. Eventually the gully became a canyon gouged so deeply into the plateau that not only was the entire flow of the eastern river diverted through it, the great inland sea began to drain into it as well, flowing north through the former inlet channel. When the huge body of water had been altogether emptied a small flow continued across its bed from the highlands to the southeast; this is the stream we call the Little Colorado River. The river that flows south down the eastern edge of the Kaibab Plateau, then arcs westward through it and turns south again at its western base to empty into the Gulf of California is the Colorado. This cycle of upthrust, erosion and river redistribution had been accomplished sometime between two and a half million and ten million years ago, and with every passing year the river has abraded deeper into the plateau, exposing layer after layer of rock that stripe the walls of its canyon course.

Three hundred feet of Kaibab Limestone forms the rim of the canyon; below that are two hundred fifty feet of the grey Toroweap Formation, three hundred feet of beige Coconino Sandstone, three hundred feet of dull, rich red Hermit Shale and a thousand feet of Supai Formation rock which, like the Hermit Shale above it, gets its heavy red color from the iron oxides it contains.

As the river continues to slice deeper into the plateau, the lips of the canyon it has created draw farther apart. The endless alternations of freeze and thaw, wind and rain, work at the layers of exposed stone, melting them back at rates which vary according to the strength or weakness of the particular stratum. The same process affects the canyons of tributary streams.

Beneath the Supai Formation is a layer of grey limestone stained red on its exposed surface by iron oxides rinsed down from the rock above. This Redwall Limestone forms sheer cliffs averaging five hundred feet in height. At the base of these cliffs are relatively small pockets of lavendar Temple Butte limestone and a four hundred foot thick layer of grey and beige Muav Formation rock. Beneath that the river has exposed a four hundred foot stratum of fine-grained greenish Bright Angel Shale which formed a broad bench as the more erosion-susceptible strata above it were nibbled back. This is the Tonto Rim, and the narrow chasm through which the river flows below is the Inner Gorge of Grand Canyon.

The river is still grinding deeper into the Vishnu Schist bedrock which underlies the present river bottom to a depth of several thousand feet, and could eventually reach a depth of nearly half a mile below its present elevation. Geologic evidence suggests that the riverbed has been excavating its channel into this bedrock at the rate of about fifty feet per million years. It is doubtful if it will continue at this rate because Glen Canyon Dam has reduced the amount of silt carried down-canyon by the current, and silt is a major abrasive agent in wearing the riverbed deeper. But even if it continued at the old rate it would require more than fifty million years to reach its maximum depth.

When that day comes, Grand Canyon will be reduced to a broad, hummocked valley through which a slow and sluggish Colorado River will meander toward the sea like a blind, forgetful old man.

[THE SOUTHERN DESERT]

For one hundred fifty years following Coronado's famous expedition of 1540, Spanish advances north from Mexico had been concentrated in the region of the Rio Grande Valley. In the last decade of the seventeenth century, however, the Spaniards began a new northern advance in the west, into what they called Pimería Alta: some fifty thousand square miles of lowlying desert lands bounded approximately by the Altar and Magdalena Rivers on the south, the San Pedro River on the east, the Gila on the north and the Colorado and the Gulf of California on the west.

Embracing parts of what is now northern Sonora and southern Arizona, the region was the home of seven major Indian tribes representing an aggregate population of perhaps thirty thousand people. These tribes were agricultural people who supplemented their crude farming by hunting and by gathering wild plants. The most numerous were the Pimas, concentrated along the upper reaches of the San Ignacio and Altar Rivers in Sonora and the Santa Cruz and San Pedro in Arizona. To the west of the Pimas along the Sonoran rivers were the Sobas, and to the north along the lower San Pedro, the Sobaipuris. Coco-maricopa villages dotted the banks of the Gila from near its bend almost to its confluence with the Colorado, which was the center of the Yuma territory. Quiquima Indians lived along the Colorado River south of the Yumas. The arid lands between the Santa Cruz and the Colorado were the home of the Papagos. Because they lacked a dependable source of water, this tribe developed an agriculture dependent upon summer rains and migrated between their cultivated fields and hunting grounds. With the exception of the Yumas, and of the Sobaipuris whose territory lay nearest to the Apaches farther east, all these tribes were relatively amiable and peaceful.

The leading figure in the Spanish entrance into Pimería Alta was an Austrian Jesuit named Eusebio Kino. In March, 1687, Kino built his first mission, Nuestra Senora de los Dolores, at an Indian village near the southern edge of Pimería Alta. By 1691 he had moved northward into what is now Arizona. No more brilliant example of the frontier missionary can be found. For more than twenty-four years he traveled among the Indian populations virtually alone and unprotected. He established twenty-four missions, stocked them with livestock and taught the Indians new techniques for farming, including the use of the metal plows he provided. He made perhaps thirty major expeditions through a region as large as the Kingdom of Portugal in which he combined ministering to the Indians with geographical exploration; it was Kino who exploded forever the old myth that California was an island, and his maps had a profound effect on exploration of the southwest for a hundred years.

To the Indians, Kino and his colleagues were clearly rich and generous magicians who represented a powerful new god. By example of his friendliness and simplicity, and by focussing his attentions on the Indian leaders who could assuage the suspicions and resentments of the general populace, Kino baptized some five thousand converts and assured a willing, though by no means universal welcome for Spanish civilization.

It has been said that the first ten years of Kino's activities among the Indians of Pimería Alta brought more change than the previous ten decades, and inevitably these rapid changes brought difficulties with them. In 1695 a Pima population on the Altar River in Sonora ambushed the Sicilian missionary there, killed him and his servants and rampaged through the small Spanish holdings, burning and looting as they went. The rebellion was quickly ended but with Kino's death in 1711 the rigors of the frontier had blunted the Spanish determination and missionary activities slackened. The nearest troop garrison was at Frontreras, about fifty miles east of the southeastern corner of Pimería Alta, and by the 1730s the only Spanish holdings in Pimería Alta besides the missions were a few ranches in the Altar and Magdelena Valleys and a small mining district near the Mission Dolores.

In 1736, however, a Yaqui Indian discovered a lode of free silver exposed on the surface of the hills southwest of the mission at Guevavi, which stood about eight miles north of present-day Nogales. Called Arizona or Arizonac, the site may explain the otherwise uncertain name later given to the state. Hundreds of prospectors from the south trekked in to explore the region; some ten thousand pounds of free silver, including a single 425-lb. "nugget" and many others nearly as large, had been taken from the shallow diggings by the time soldiers arrived to protect the king's interest in the find.

This sudden increase in Spanish activity on the frontier coincided with an increase in the Indian revulsion toward the changes forty years of Spanish occupation had brought. Many of these changes had been beneficial, particularly the advanced agricultural tools and techniques. But the Spanish gifts of chol-

era, Christianity, military conscription and forced labor were hardly welcomed. What had been an amiable, industrious population in Kino's day had become "a rabble of drunkards and reprobates," more and more of whom had to be forcibly removed from their villages to maintain the mission work forces.

In 1751 a troop of Pimas recruited for a scouting raid against the Apaches turned on the Spaniards, killing a pair of priests and perhaps as many as a hundred Spanish settlers while destroying the missions at Tubac and Arivaca and driving the Spanish military south. Early the following year a force of eighty-six Spanish soldiers defeated two thousand Pima warriors and restored an uneasy peace by establishing a presidio at Tubac.

In the 1760s neophyte desertions from the missions and their deaths from disease had created a severe labor shortage at the missions. To correct it, the missionaries made the catastrophic mistake of relocating the Sobaipuris from their San Pedro River villages to the missions. Without the Sobaipuris to act as a buffer the Santa Cruz Valley lay unprotected against the Apaches; raiders at once swept into the valley in a furious series of attacks. By the end of the decade the combination of disease, alcoholism and Apache raiding had virtually destroyed the Pima people for whom the region had been named.

In 1776 a new Spanish presidio was established at Tucson, a visita of the old Kino mission at Bac, and by 1800 a new Spanish posture of conciliation and generosity toward the Apaches had nearly eliminated Spanish raiding altogether. With the outbreak of the Mexican War for Independence, however, this policy could no longer be maintained and by the early 1830s Apache raiding parties were roaming the countryside almost at will. So ferocious and unremitting were their attacks that Tubac was abandoned in 1848, leaving Tucson as the only non-Indian settlement in what is now Arizona.

Tucson by this time had already accumulated an eventful history. As the fortified redoubt to which the settlers in the Santa Cruz Valley fled at the approach of the Apaches, Tucson had twice been besieged by Apache armies of more than a thousand warriors. Mexican independence resulted in a dwindling of population in the town, though the troops stationed there continued to fight the Apaches as best they could under the nearly impossible conditions imposed upon them. And in 1846 these harassed troops were called upon to face a new challenge.

With the outbreak of the Mexican War, Kearny's "Army of the West" had marched into New Mexico, occupied it without firing a shot, and moved on with the bulk of his

force to California. In addition to the Missourians he left as garrison troops in New Mexico, Kearny also detached the Mormon Battalion to invade Arizona. Marching west from Socorro, New Mexico in late autumn, the Battalion faced its first engagement in the valley of the San Pedro River where they were surprised not by Mexican soldiers or Apaches, but by a herd of enraged longhorn cattle. In the melee the Mormons suffered three casualties, the colonel in command, who himself, was nearly gored, referred to the "skirmish" in his journals as "the battle of bull run."

A more serious confrontation seemed imminent when scouts reported the Mexican force at Tucson preparing for resistance. As the Americans approached, however, messengers brought word that the defenders' orders required only that resistance be offered to prevent the Americans from taking the settlement, and that if they would circle around the place on their way west nothing would be done to interfere with them. This offer was refused and the Mexican surrender demanded. Surrender was declined and on December 16th the American force had moved to within sight of the fortified village.

No sooner had they done so than word was brought from Tucson that the Mexican troops were withdrawing to the south, and after waiting for a discrete interval the Americans calmly took possession. The Mormon Battalion lingered two days in Tucson before resuming the westward march by way of the Santa Cruz and the Gila to the Colorado, then across the Imperial Valley to San Diego. Their route, the Gila Trail, became a fairly popular route to California during the Gold Rush three years later.

The treaty of Guadalupe Hidalgo ended the Mexican War—and the early period of Arizona history—before word of the California gold discoveries had trickled east, and Arizona (then considered a part of New Mexico) was ceded to the United States. The Joint boundary commission which began the survey to determine the new international boundary line in the summer of 1849 quickly discovered that the map upon which the treaty had been based was in error. Disagreement led to squabbling and squabbling led to disintegration of the survey attempt. In 1853 James Gadsden was dispatched to Mexico City to negotiate the compromise purchase by which the United States acquired land south of the Gila.

In that same year a party of Americans from the California gold fields found evidence of silver in the slopes above the Santa Cruz Valley, and by 1856 a mining corporation capitalized at a million dollars had begun operations there with its headquarters in the old Spanish presidio at Tubac. In the summer of 1858 Sylvester Mowry had put another mine into operation, and in that year, too, a placer gold strike had been made about twenty miles above the mouth of the Gila River. By 1861 there were several hundred miners at Gila City earning, reportedly, from $30 to $120 a day.

News of these and other more ephemeral finds drew more and more Americans to the southern Arizona deserts, to the considerable consternation of the Apaches. Their mountain strongholds extended from the Chiricahua and Dragoon ranges in the southeast to the Superstitions near the center of the state and from them they had been accustomed to raiding the valley settlements since long before the arrival of the Spaniards. The Apache attitude toward the Americans—few of whom dared to venture within the Apache territory itself—was a mixture of annoyance and respect, and several of their leading men, among them Cochise, began to confine their raids mostly across the border into Mexico.

The Mexicans understandably resented the fact that Apache raiders from the United States ravaged their farms and slaughtered their neighbors and then fled to sanctuary across the border. They began to retaliate by stealing American cattle and driving them surreptitiously into Mexico to replace the animals stolen by the Apaches.

The growing bitterness along the border was accelerated wildly in 1861 when a young lieutenant from the garrison near Tucson was detailed to investigate the theft of a small band of cattle and the kidnapping of a six year old boy by an Apache raiding party. The lieutenant managed to make contact with Cochise at Apache Pass and demanded the return of the boy and the animals. Cochise denied any knowledge of the affair but offered to attempt to find the missing boy and the cattle and to help arrange for their return. The lieutenant, apparently under the misconception that Cochise was some manner of dictator with full authority over all Apaches, called him a liar and arrested him with his companions. Cochise escaped by slashing through the tent and loping off into the night, but six other Apaches were captured and held as hostages.

Cochise retaliated by taking a number of prisoners of his own and demanded an exchange. When this was refused he ordered his captives tortured; with the discovery of their deaths, the six Apaches were hanged from a tree. All Apache restraint on the American side of the border ended at once. Ranches were plundered and burned, cattle

herds driven into the mountains and travelers were slaughtered on sight.

And almost simultaneously the Army troops departed Fort Buchanan near Tucson for Civil War duty leaving the Apaches in utter control of all of southern Arizona save the two tiny fortified enclaves at Tucson and Fort Yuma. The mining offices at Tubac were abandoned and the workings closed down, but Sylvester Mowry fortified his diggings against attack and even managed to maintain a limited production of ore which he stockpiled against the time he would be able to transport it to a mill. The Butterfield Stage, which had connected with the Pacific coast through Tucson since 1858, was discontinued; Gila City was abandoned, though not because of the danger of Indian attack. The gold there had given out, and a journalist visiting the place three years later noted that "the promising metropolis of Arizona consisted of three chimneys and a coyote."

The small American population at Tucson had come principally from the southern states. But it was largely because the rebel force invading New Mexico offered the most readily available source of protection against the Apaches that Arizona declared for the Confederacy. A separate "Territory of Arizona" was proclaimed by the Confederacy— the long, narrow strip between the thirty-fourth parallel and the Mexican border—with its capital at Mesilla, and a delegate to the rebel Congress was elected at Tucson and sent to Richmond.

Union resistance to the Confederate occupation of the southwest crystalized at Fort Craig, New Mexico, some one hundred twenty miles up the Rio Grande from Colonel John Baylor's rebel force at Mesilla, and soon 2,500 federal troops had gathered there. From Texas, Brigadier H. H. Sibley led his "Army of New Mexico," consisting of three regiments of cavalry, to Mesilla where he incorporated Baylor's force into his own and moved north against the federal positions at Val Verde outside Fort Craig. In mid-February, 1862, he attacked the Union line and drove the enemy from their positions. Instead of laying siege to Fort Craig, however, Sibley moved north to capture Santa Fe, the capital of Confederate New Mexico.

Sibley also sent a small detachment to garrison Tucson. They were welcomed warmly and took what action they could against the Apaches. On a patrol through the Indian villages along the Gila, a small troop of rebel soldiers encountered an even smaller foraging party from Fort Yuma and took them prisoners. Not long afterward a larger force of Union troops was ordered to clear the Yuma-Tucson road. The 13-man scouting de-

tachment preceding the main body of troops was ambushed by fifteen Confederate soldiers at Picacho Peak, and in the sudden skirmish that resulted three of the federal soldiers were killed, including the lieutenant. Two rebels were killed and three more captured, but the westernmost "battle" of the Civil War was considered a Confederate victory because they drove the Union force into retreat. Despite this "victory" the Confederates soon abandoned Tucson and moved quickly to rejoin the main rebel force along the Rio Grande; they were badly mauled by Apaches in the process.

In June, 1862, Union troops entered Tucson from the west, proclaimed the United States Territory of Arizona (with the same boundaries as the Confederate Territory), and began levying taxes. Sylvester Mowry was imprisoned at Fort Yuma for six months and found his mine looted of its high-grade ore upon his release.

General Sibley, meanwhile, was having his troubles in New Mexico. After an abortive attack against the Union forces in which his wagons and stores were captured, he found himself menaced by the simultaneous advance of federal troops from Arizona and Missouri, and he retreated to Texas. The Army of New Mexico, about half its number killed, captured or incapacitated during its long southwestern campaign, had never lost a battle but could not keep Arizona and New Mexico for the Confederacy. The Union forces in Arizona linked up with those in New Mexico and pressed the attack against Sibley in Texas.

With the southwestern Territories cleared of Confederate troops, military action was once again directed against the Apaches, and settlers began to brave the grazing lands beyond sight of Tucson. Ranching became profitable, though still precarious, and mining swelled Arizona's population substantially. Gold discoveries had been made at several points along the Colorado before the war and prospectors flooded along the banks of the river to look for more. Strikes were made at La Paz, Olive City and Ehrenburg and flourishing settlements grew up around them. This series of discoveries, along with the restoration of production at the mines established before the war, encouraged Congress to create the Territory of Arizona, establishing the boundaries that still enclose the state, but also including a vast tract of desert land west of the Colorado which now makes up most of Clark County, Nevada. The Territorial legislature met for the first time in 1864 near the location of half a dozen rich mines, at a struggling settlement named Prescott.

For the rest of the decade Arizona's non-Indian population grew steadily despite the increasingly desperate Apache resistance. Reservations had been established, and though they were little more than concentration camps, they did offer refuge from the relentless Army troops, and Indians were accepting them. Often enough, however, Indians who had spent a period of recuperation at the reservation would slip away again to resume raiding.

In 1871 one such band under the leadership of Eskiminzin surrendered to the Army at Fort Grant and asked to return to the reservation. While the request was relayed to the proper authority the Apaches were given rations, blankets and permission to settle themselves outside the post. Other Apaches joined Eskiminzin's waiting band and their numbers increased to about three hundred.

While this was taking place another Apache party made a raid at Tubac, making off with some horses and committing other outrages against the ranchers there. The settlers placed blame for the affair on Eskiminzin's Apaches despite denials by Eskiminzin and by the Army. Mass meetings held in Tucson resulted in appeals for justice being sent to the commander of the Arizona Department who refused to act.

Burning with indignation, six Americans and ninety-two vengeful Papagos slipped in small groups to a rendezvous where a wagonload of weapons was waiting, and from there to a bluff overlooking the Indian encampment. At dawn they slaughtered virtually every man woman and child.

When word of the massacre reached the press the incident became a national outrage. The killers, freely admitting what they had done, were brought to trial in Tucson and acquitted: no one in that long-beleaguered settlement would convict a man of killing Apaches under any circumstances.

The incident resulted in a change in the federal policy toward the Apaches from subjugation to negotiation and within eighteen months about half of the previously hostile tribes had voluntarily entered reservations. In 1872 General O. O. Howard met with Cochise in his Chiricahua Mountain stronghold and made a treaty of peace. Such was Cochise's character that the Apaches, over whom he had no authority except the respect in which he was held, lived up to the treaty without incident.

With Cochise's death in 1874, however, Geronimo, one of his ablest and most belligerent lieutenants broke away and fled across the border into Mexico's Sierra Madre Mountains. From there he raided unmercifully, was

captured and released in 1877, and finally induced to surrender with the remnants of his band in 1886. After a period of confinement in Florida, Geronimo earned a sparse living as an exhibit in middle western state and county fairs and by selling picture postcards of himself.

Even before Geronimo's capture, however, the Apache strongholds in southeastern Arizona had been invaded. Ed Scheiffelin's discovery of silver near the foot of the Dragoon Mountains had attracted more than seven thousand miners, saloonkeepers, merchants, shady ladies and hangers-on to the city that grew up to serve the mines: Tombstone.

Hard cases like Johnny Ringo, Bat Masterson, the Earp brothers and Buckskin Frank Leslie made a reputation for Tombstone that were to become the basis of more fortunes made in Hollywood than from all the mines of the Tombstone district put together.

The Tombstone excitement also drew ranchers and farmers to feed the miners, and the opening of the country to settlement in spite of the Apaches marked the practical end of their menace. But Tombstone was also the last stand of the prospecting miner. By the turn of the century, with the exhaustion of most of Arizona's precious metal mines, most of the rapidly increasing mineral production was the work of corporations, and most importantly the copper mining corporations. The Ajo copper mines a short distance north of the Mexican border in southwestern Arizona had been in production since 1854. In 1875 the Arizona Copper Company began operations in the Metcalf-Clifton-Morenci region near the New Mexico border, and a major discovery was made at Bisbee near the Mexican border in the southeast. Copper mining began on a large scale at Globe in 1878 and at Jerome, overlooking the Verde Valley, ten years later. By 1900 Arizona was producing more than half the nation's domestic copper.

Texas ranchers, bankrupt and landless in the aftermath of the Civil War, had moved the remnants of their herds to Arizona and to other western states in the 1870s; by the 1880s with the decline of the Apaches enormous herds were grazing the grasslands of the southeast and of the Mogollon Rim country far to the north. Barbed wire ended the era of the open range in the 1890s but the windmill pump opened the country, to less hardy but more profitable breeds than the Texas longhorn only a few years later.

From the turn of the century until World War I Arizona grew slowly on the foundations laid in the century preceding: mining, livestock and agriculture; in February, 1912,

Arizona became the forty-eighth state. The unique landscapes and clear, dry climate had been attracting visitors since two transcontinental railroads were completed across the Territory in the early 1880s, and their numbers increased dramatically as automobile travel made Arizona more readily accessible to an increasingly mobile population of Americans. But it was with World War II and its aftermath that Arizona boomed with unprecedented development and prosperity.

The state's location away from the coast but near to the California military bases and transportation prompted the location of war-related industry in Arizona, increasing gross manufacturing revenues from $17 million in 1940 to $85 million in 1945, an increase of four hundred per cent. Air bases were located in the state to take advantage of the excellent flying conditions available most days of the year for training pilots, and Army units were trained in desert tactics. By the end of the war, Phoenix and Tucson had nearly doubled in size, and in the fifteen years from 1945 to 1960 the state as a whole increased 111 per cent in population and in income nearly three hundred per cent. Phoenix, a hay camp less than a century before, had become the fastest growing city in America.

This staggering rate of growth, while it has provided substantial material benefits to the state and its people, has also brought difficulties. Some of the problems are the social problems long familiar in other parts of the country, the product of disrupted traditions, the industrialization of a rural region and the increasing density of urban population. But in Arizona these problems assume a special urgency, for they rest upon an even more profound difficulty: water. The Salt River Project, though it provides enough water to serve New York City, is no longer adequate to meet the needs of central Arizona. The Central Arizona Project has now been authorized to bring water from the Colorado River east into the central farm lands. At the same time, forest scientists are working energetically to devise methods for wringing every available drop of water from the highland watersheds without destroying their forest ecologies. Yet each success in providing more water re-creates the problem in larger dimension by spurring more growth. Despite the characteristic Arizona energy and determination, in spite of advances in science and technology, the water problem faced by Arizona is essentially that which has faced every people who have dwelt in the magnificent expanses of the southern desert. It makes the question of what happened to the Hohokam seem ever more important.

Right: Autumn's brilliant colors reflected on crystal-clear Bog Creek, Fort Apache Indian Reservation.

Below: West fork of the Black River flows down the slopes of White Mountains, Apache National Forest.

Right: Autumn's delicate transition along the snow-covered banks of the Blue River in White Mountains.

Below: White River cuts through volcanic gorge near Fort Apache. Historic post was established in 1870.

Right: Grass and golden aspen leaves create a textured pattern on forest pond in White Mountains.

Below: Western yellow pine depicts life and death aside a sturdy log cabin under a threatening summer sky. Viewed near Big Lake on State Highway 273.

Right: Lonely fence in White Mountain volcanic field near Springerville. On pages 36 and 37 following: Sandstone pillars in Monument Valley from left to right: Bear and Rabbit, Cathedral Butte, and King on his Throne. South from base of Brigham's tomb.

Below: Morning sun silhouettes Yebechai Rocks in Monument Valley. In foreground, a Navajo home.

Right: Arid desert prevailed as a Juniper lost the fight for survival. In the background, Yebechai rock formations. Monument Valley, Navajo Tribal Park.

Below: A brilliant sun highlights the evening sky over Eagle Mesa in Monument Valley, Navajo Tribal Park.

Right: Shade ramada, Navajo summer home, dwarfed at base of Agathla (El Capitan), a giant volcanic plug.

Below: Parade of sandstone monoliths reflect King-on-Throne, Stagecoach, Bear and Rabbit on desert pool in the Monument Valley, Navajo Tribal Park.

Right: Sage and sand create informal relationship. In background, Three Sisters rocks in Navajo land.

Below: Poncho House, an Anasazi ruins along Chinle Wash. In the distance, glimpse of Monument Valley.

Right: Sunset highlights face of Stagecoach, Bear and Rabbit rocks, Monument Valley, Navajo Tribal Park.

Right: Wind-whipped sands create an interesting ripple pattern near Sand Springs in Monument Valley.

Below: Looking north from the base of Thunderbird Mesa into wide, arid expanse of Monument Valley.

Right: Echo cave ruin remains standing as monument of excellence to its builders in Navajo Indian land.

Below: View northeast from high atop Hunt's Mesa.
Evening sun on sandstone formations in the valley.

Right: Sandstone Buttes of Monument Valley from
right to left: Big Indian, West Mitten and Three Sisters. On pages 52 and 53 following: Sunset renders
an aura of mystery and drama to a broad expanse of
Monument Valley. View north from Hunt's Mesa.

Below: Piercing midday sun and summer clouds portray one of many shifting moods in Monument Valley.

Right: Ear of the Wind in Monument Valley. Plateau winds and rain formed window in Wingate sandstone.

Below: Organ Pipe and Saguaro cacti are numerous in lower Sonoran desert. In background, Tillotson Peak along Ajo Mountain Drive, Organ Pipe Cactus National Monument. It spans an area of 516 miles.

Right: Nearly upright stems of Organ Pipe cactus frame the stately Saguaro in Ajo Mountain Range. The Saguaro, or giant cactus will reach a height of forty feet, the Organ Pipe, twenty-five feet.

Below: Giant Chain Cholla and Jojoba bush amidst a carpet of Mexican Poppy. Background, Sierra del Ajo (elevation 4843 feet), Organ Pipe Cactus Monument.

Right: Organ Pipe cactus from which the National Monument received its name. It is the home of 31 species of cactus and 225 kinds of birds. In the distance are the Cubabi Mountains of Sonora, Mexico.

Below: Clay soil erodes beneath huge log that fell 200,000,000 years ago. Petrified Forest National Park.

Right: Centuries of erosion exposed this log to form natural bridge in Petrified Forest National Park. Discovered in 1851, area was designated a park in 1962.

Below: Wood fragments that started as living trees in a prehistoric forest. They are preserved by silica and dyed beautifully by iron oxide and magnesium.

Right: Chinle formations eroded by wind and rain in Petrified Forest National Park. In foreground, petrified log caps a small clay ridge which will eventually crumble. As old ridges continue to crumble, new ones begin forming beneath the fallen log fragments.

Below: Looking north from Kachina Point into the vast expanse of Painted Desert, Petrified Forest Park.

Right: Notes on Newspaper Rock can't be read today. These petroglyphs on varnished sandstone may have had religious significance, Petrified Forest Park.

Below: A Century Plant adapts to the volcanic rock in Peralta Canyon, Superstition Mountain Wilderness.

Right: Desert tank in upper Peralta Canyon along Superstition Wilderness Trail. Background, Picket Post Mountains. It is rich experience for the hiker.

Below: Boles of Saguaro dwarf the little fishhook and the prickly pear cacti growing at their base.

Right: Cholla, Saguaro cacti and whiplike Ocotillo are natives of the Sonoran Desert. In background are volcanic remnants of the Superstition Mountains.

Right: Midday sun highlights chain-fruit Cholla 'at base
of volcanic Superstition Mountains east of Phoenix.

Below: Beavertail cactus and Brittlebrush give the arid Sonoran Desert a pleasant splash of color in April. In background is 4877 foot Kofa Mountain.

Right: Sunlight gives varnished look to black walls of Kofa Mountains. Foreground, Ocotillo, Brittlebrush.

Below: Autumn foliage delivers a brilliant splash of poetic color in Oak Creek Canyon south of Flagstaff.

Right: Ponderosa pine seems determined to survive on wall of petrified dunes in Oak Creek Canyon.

Below: Chapel of the Holy Cross near Sedona in Oak Creek Canyon. The red rock cliffs blend in perfect harmony with this memorial Chapel built in 1956.

Right: Sun pierces storm to illuminate red rock formations above Oak Creek Canyon on Schnebly Hill.

Below: Camera captures unusual bark design on a trunk of an Arizona Cypress in Oak Creek Canyon.

Right: Oak Creek flows over sandstone strata just below Slide Rock. On pages 84 and 85 following: Winter sunrise touches ramparts above Sedona in Oak Creek Canyon. Viewed from Schnebly Hill Road.

Below: The erosion-carved buttes and forested land surround Sedona, the gateway to Oak Creek Canyon.

Right: Sunlight envelops a grove of Ponderosa pine in upper Oak Creek Canyon, Coconino National Forest.

Below: Grand Falls on the Little Colorado River. Heavy summer rains were responsible for this scene.

Right: October blooming Rabbitbrush adapts to the gentle clay slopes of Chinle Wash near Many Farms.

Below: Shinarump conglomerate boulder in perfect balance near Lee's Ferry. In the distance, Echo Cliffs.

Right: Cottonwoods herald the coming of spring in upper Navajo Canyon near Inscription House ruin.

Below: View across Lake Powell to the sun drenched cliffs of Utah. Glen Canyon National Recreation Area.

Right: Erosion carved faces in Entrada sandstone on Babyrocks Mesa near Kayenta on Navajo Reservation.

Below: A late afternoon sun dramatically silhouettes Mojave yucca in the Detrital Valley near Kingman.

Right: Weather-worn wall in Chloride appears structurally sound in this arid region. In background, silver mine and tailings at base of Cerbat Mountains.

Right: Winter's generous mantle adorns Cholla and Yucca in Detrital Valley. Black Mountains on horizon.

Below: Morning sun adds sparkle to delicate snow laden yucca in Cerbat Mountains north of Kingman.

Right: Satin smooth Mooney Falls makes a dramatic drop into turquoise tinted waters of Havasu Creek.

Below: Early morning solar reflection on the mirror-like surface of Canyon Lake northeast of Phoenix.

Right: Orange Mexican Poppy, Owl Clover and Lupine carpet this hillside along the Apache Trail. In background, giant Saguaro stands as a silent sentinel.

Below: Morning sun highlights snow on Bonito lava flow in Sunset Crater National Monument near U.S. 89.

Right: Winter storms are a peril to survival in ancient Bristlecone pine forest on the San Francisco Peaks.

Below: Low hanging clouds envelop Sunset Crater. In foreground, naked aspen await Spring amidst somber conifers on the slopes of Bonito lava flow.

Right: The brilliant Arizona Rocket or scarlet Gillia grows on cinder slopes of extinct Sunset Crater.

Below: Bleached roots of Bistlecone Pine below timberline on the volcanic slopes of Agassiz Peak.

Right: Snowcaps on a blanket of cinders and ash in 3000 acre Sunset Crater National Monument on horizon are the San Francisco Peaks obscured by clouds.

Below: A thick stand of quaking aspen lends brilliant contrast to Humphrey's Peak. Aspen saplings grow in dense sibling stands at the rate of about a foot a year.

Right: White aspen boles form a dense grove on the south face of San Francisco Peaks, Coconino Forest.

Below: Engelmann Spruce and grass thickly encrusted with frost and snow, Coconino National Forest.

Right: An abundance of vegetation adapts to the volcanic slopes of Merriam Crater east of Flagstaff.

Below: Winter's generous mantle gracefully adorns stand of Ponderosa pine in Kaibab National Forest.

Right: Ponderosa pine trees seem well adapted on Bonito lava flow. Sunset Crater National Monument. On pages 116 and 117 following: San Francisco Mountains dominated by Humphrey's Peak (elevation 12,670 feet). It is the highest point in Arizona. In foreground the San Francisco volcanic field.

Below: Wukoki ruin occupied by Pueblo Indians during the 12th and 13th century, Wupatki National Monument. In the distance are San Francisco Peaks.

Right: Morning sun casts interesting shadows of lava rock and sand grass along shore of Little Colorado.

Below: Grasses and Rabbitbrush contrast against the volcanic cinder field in Wupatki National Monument.

Right: Groups of Teddy bear Cholla and Saguaro on desert near Aguila. Background, Harcuvar Mountains.

Below: Wupatki ruin (Wupatki is a Hopi word meaning tall house). This multistoried ruin containing some 100 rooms was occupied during the 13th century.

Right: Vertical limestone cliff shelters Montezuma Castle occupied by ancient Sinagua Indians in the 13th Century. This cliff dwelling of five stories and twenty rooms is preserved in a National Monument.

Right: Eroded volcanic formations and balanced rocks seemingly construct a maze of fairytale figures in the Chiricahua National Monument, Cochise County.

Below: Saguaro cacti silhouette against a brilliant sunset and summer thundershower in Saguaro National Monument. Background, Roskruge Mountains.

Right: Hedgehog cactus provides a splash of color on Sonoran Desert near base of Harcuvar Mountains.

Below: The large Prickly pear cactus dwarfs the April blooming Hedgehog at base of Harcuvar Mountains.

Right: Rose-purple cups of Hedgehog cactus in early April, a sign of springtime on the Sonoran Desert.

Below: Giant Dagger yuccas dominate plants in Gila River Valley. In the background, Pinaleno Mountains.

Right: Cottonwood tree robed with autumn foliage along Sonoita Creek tributary of the Santa Cruz River. On pages 132 and 133 following: Carpet of Dune Primrose and Sand Verbena on Mojave Desert.

Below: Saguaro edge the desert in Saguaro National Monument near Tucson. Yonder Quinlan Mountains.

Right: Gila polychrome pot made during the 15th century. A museum piece at University of Arizona.

Below: Dense community of Saguaro cacti in Tucson Mountain Park. Its blossom is Arizona's state flower.

Right: A rare moisture laden fog lies beyond a Teddy bear Cholla colony in Saguaro National Monument.

Below: Floodlighted Mission San Xavier del Bac on San Xavier Indian Reservation, serving the Papago Indians since it was founded in 1692. The present church has been in use since 1797. In the distance, lights of Tucson at base of the Santa Catalina Range.

Right: Sabino Creek flows from alpine forests through Saguaro dotted slopes, Santa Catalina Mountains.

Right: Giant boulders in Sabino Creek form placid pools and delicate falls in Santa Catalina Mountains.

Below: The evening sun highlights a forest of young Saguaro cacti and Ocotillo in Saguaro Monument.

Right: Symbolic Saguaro silhouettes downtown Tucson. Santa Catalina Mountains dominate the horizon.

Below: Downtown Phoenix skyline reflects the tremendous growth of this major metropolis. In the distance rugged peaks of the Camelback Mountains.

Right: Acres of maize growing in fertile Valley of the Sun, near Phoenix. Background, fan palm trees.

Below: Modern residence halls and palm trees along campus boulevard, Arizona State University, Tempe.

Right: Dome shaped Fishhook cactus dominates the broken remnants of rock on the desert floor in the Superstition Wilderness Area. On pages 148 and 149 following: Temple of Isis viewed from the south rim at Mather Point in Grand Canyon National Park.

Below: Situated in the granite gorge of the Colorado River is gleaming fluted Vishnu Schist, one of the oldest layers of exposed rock known to man. It is so ancient that there is no definite clue as to its origin.

Right: Forces of erosion etched the sandstone strata along Colorado River, Grand Canyon National Park.

Below: Massive lava boulders strew the path and edge the banks of surging turbulent Colorado River.

Right: Carving its way through Tapeats sandstone is crystal-clear Deer Creek in Kaibab National Forest.

Below: Colorado River through Marble Canyon, longest, wildest, most exciting waterway in the world.

Right: The Colorado River seems tame as it passes through Furnace Flats rimmed by rugged basalt cliffs.

Below: Elves' chasm on Royal Arch Creek, tributary of the Colorado River, Grand Canyon National Park.

Right: Brilliant sunrise drenches a limestone cathedral, reflected on Colorado River in Marble Canyon.

Below: Vulcan's Throne (elevation 5108 feet), a once active volcano sending flow of lava across Colorado River, creating Lava Falls Rapids. In the foreground, lone Sotol struggles for a foothold in sandstone rim.

Right: Colorado River appears as a silver ribbon in the Grand Canyon. View is from Toroweap Overlook.

Below: Ponderosa pine grove in the Kaibab National Forest. White-tailed Kaibab squirrel, a species found nowhere else in the world, roams this lofty forest.

Right: On the Kaibab plateau flaming autumn colors light the quaking aspens in Kaibab National Forest.

Below: View from Point Imperial on the North Rim in early morning. In foreground, Mount Hayden depicts the enormous depth of this mighty canyon.

Right: Looking south from Bright Angel Point, the evening sun highlights Deva Temple, Angel's Gate, South Rim and the distant San Francisco Peaks. On pages 164 and 165 following: View north through limestone arch into expanse of the Grand Canyon.

Below: Streaking sun delineates massive space of this layered rim country, Grand Canyon National Park.

Right: On the North Rim, Angel's Window brings into view turbulent Unkar Rapids on Colorado River.

Below: Autumn tinted aspen in upper Bright Angel Canyon relieve the somber cast of a conifer forest.

Right: Mather Point view on the South Rim. In the distance is sunlit tip of Isis Temple and the North Rim.

Below: White fir near Jacob Lake (elevation 7921 ft.) thickly encrusted with snow, Kaibab National Forest.

Right: It is over 4000 feet down from Hopi Point to Hermit Rapids of the Colorado River. In foreground, the brilliant June blooming Claret Cup and Yucca.

Below: Indian ruins abandoned in 13th century. In 1930 they were completely excavated by University of Arizona archaeologists, Tuzigoot National Monument.

Right: Huge slablike layers of sandstone anchor Anasazi ruins in Monument Valley Navajo Tribal Park.

Below: Cochise County Courthouse in historic Tombstone, completed in 1882 at a cost of $50,000. In foreground, yuccas slowly cover silver mine tailings.

Right: Eroding facade on Cleopatra's Hill in Jerome. In distance San Francisco Peaks above Verde Valley.

Below: Old well and abandoned buildings in Gleeson near the town of Tombstone in Cochise County.

Right: Partially restored ruin of Mission San Jose de Tumacacori near Tubac, established in 1691. It is centered in a region rich in Spanish colonial history.

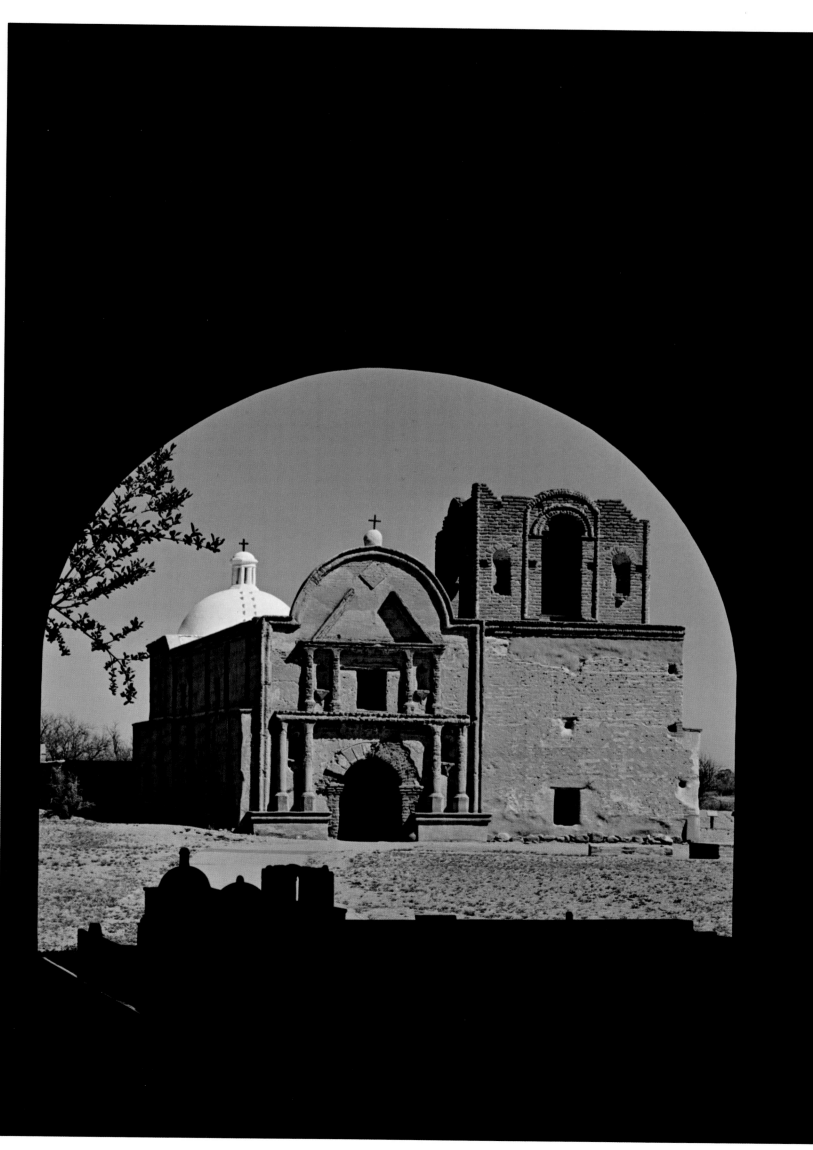

Below: Barrel cactus along Pinal Pioneer Parkway midway between Florence and Oracle Junction.

Right: Bristlecone Pine on Agassiz Peak has withstood the ravages of winter for over 2000 years.

Below: December can be dazzlingly bright on Cerbat Mountain Range. In foreground, the Mojave Yucca.

Right: Navajo farm on the floor of Canyon de Chelly (de Shay) National Monument. The sheer cliffs dropping suddenly from the surrounding uplands offer breathtaking views of this spectacular sandy wash.

Below: A rare desert daisy lends a lively splash of color to rock-laden Arizona shoreline of Lake Mead.

Right: Nolina renders brilliant contrast to the rugged slopes of Black Mountains. View from Sitgreaves Pass.

Below: Desert buckwheat in autumn bloom, anchors slopes below the Vermilion Cliffs, near Lee's Ferry.

Right: Contrasting autumn leaves and metamorphic rock along Sabino Creek in Santa Catalina Mountains.

Below: Acres of winter lettuce in Valley of the Sun near Phoenix. In background, Camelback Mountains.

Right: Spectacular Grand Canyon labyrinth on the Colorado River at mile 155 just above Havasu Canyon.

Ten years is less than the blink of an eye
compared with the unfettered eons that are
represented in the profound, almost
supernatural beauty of the Arizona landscape.
In the course of this brief cosmic moment,
as I was making the collection of photographs
which appears in this book, I have seen the
blazing cinerama sky smudged increasingly
with the murk of progress. If this is allowed
to continue, a few people will benefit
materially while the rest of us—and the
earth itself—are brought closer to bankruptcy.

DAVID MUENCH